DON'T GIVE ME NO BOILED OKRA

(I DON'T WANT NOTH'IN IN MY MOUTH THAT MY TEETH CAN'T ENJOY FIRST)

By: Gerald L. Cooper

THE CIRCUIT RIDER COMEDIAN

To: John & Elaine
Gerald L. Cooper

DON'T GIVE ME NO BOILED OKRA
(I DON'T WANT NOTH'IN IN MY MOUTH
THAT MY TEETH CAN'T ENJOY FIRST)

Copyright © 2013 by Gerald L. Cooper

ISBN: 978-0-9962706-0-1

All rights reserved. No part of this book may be reproduced or transmitted in any form or by any means, electronic or mechanical, including photocopying, recording, or by any information storage or retrieval system, without written permission from the author, except for brief quotations in reviews.

Scriptures taken from the Holy Bible, New International Version®, NIV®. Copyright © 1973, 1978, 1984, 2011 by Biblica, Inc.™ Used by permission of Zondervan. All rights reserved worldwide. www.zondervan.com The "NIV" and "New International Version" are trademarks registered in the United States Patent and Trademark Office by Biblica, Inc.™

The author has taken all reasonable measures to give credit where credit is due to prevent any possible copyright infringements.

Any trademarks contained herein are the property of their respective owners.

DEDICATION

This book is dedicated to my daughters,
Rebecca (Becca) Reed and Elizabeth Blankenbeckler,
and to my granddaughters Jacey and Kylie Reed.

IN LOVING MEMORY

ROSCOE

"MY LITTLE BUDDY"

March 22, 2005 – February 26, 2015

REST IN PEACE

TABLE OF CONTENTS

ACKNOWLEDGEMENTS..vii

FOREWORD xi

CHAPTER ONE
IT'S ONLY LAURIE! 1

CHAPTER TWO
SALSBERRY STEAK IN THE CAN 11

CHAPTER THREE
HERE COMES THE BEARS! 21

CHAPTER FOUR
I'LL WHOOP YOU IF YOU DO AND THEY SAID THEY WOULD TOO! 31

CHAPTER FIVE
πr^2 (Pi – r^2) {PIE ARE SQUARE} 39

CHAPTER SIX
WE WEREN'T LOST; WE JUST WENT THE WRONG WAY 45

CHAPTER SEVEN
STEVEN: THE ONE THEY STONED BACK TO LIFE 53

CHAPTER EIGHT
WHO SAID I LIKED LASAGNA? 63

CHAPTER NINE
DON'T FORGET THE HOTDOG! 69

CHAPTER TEN
HAND PRINT ON THE FACE 77

CHAPTER ELEVEN
THAT'S MY DADDY! 85

CHAPTER TWELVE
WHAT A FART! 93

CHAPTER THIRTEEN
DON'T LICK YOUR PRIVATE PARTS AND THEN TRY TO LICK MY FACE, THEN WE HAVE A DEAL. (THE STORY ON HOW I GOT MY DOG) 101

CHAPTER FOURTEEN
PLEASE FLUSH! 111

CHAPTER FIFTEEN
TINA – YOU MIGHT WANT TO EXPLAIN THAT! 119

CHAPTER SIXTEEN
YOU MIGHT JUST HAVE THE CALLING YOU MIGHT NOT BE READY FOR YOUR CALLING 131

CHAPTER SEVENTEEN
I DON'T CARE WHAT YOU PLAY, YOU GET THEM IN AND YOU GET THEM OUT! THAT'S AN ORDER!! 137

CLOSING 147
INDEX 149

TABLE OF CONTENTS

ACKNOWLEDGEMENTS vii

FOREWORD xi

CHAPTER ONE
    IT'S ONLY LAURIE! 1

CHAPTER TWO
    SALSBERRY STEAK IN THE CAN 11

CHAPTER THREE
    HERE COMES THE BEARS! 21

CHAPTER FOUR
    I'LL WHOOP YOU IF YOU DO
    AND THEY SAID THEY WOULD TOO! 31

CHAPTER FIVE
    πr^2 *(Pi – r^2) {PIE ARE SQUARE}* 39

CHAPTER SIX
    WE WEREN'T LOST; WE JUST WENT THE WRONG WAY 45

CHAPTER SEVEN
    STEVEN: THE ONE THEY STONED BACK TO LIFE 53

CHAPTER EIGHT
    WHO SAID I LIKED LASAGNA? 63

CHAPTER NINE
DON'T FORGET THE HOTDOG! 69

CHAPTER TEN
HAND PRINT ON THE FACE 77

CHAPTER ELEVEN
THAT'S MY DADDY! 85

CHAPTER TWELVE
WHAT A FART! 93

CHAPTER THIRTEEN
DON'T LICK YOUR PRIVATE PARTS AND THEN
TRY TO LICK MY FACE, THEN WE HAVE A DEAL.
(THE STORY ON HOW I GOT MY DOG) 101

CHAPTER FOURTEEN
PLEASE FLUSH! 111

CHAPTER FIFTEEN
TINA – YOU MIGHT WANT TO EXPLAIN THAT! 119

CHAPTER SIXTEEN
YOU MIGHT JUST HAVE THE CALLING
YOU MIGHT NOT BE READY FOR YOUR CALLING 131

CHAPTER SEVENTEEN
I DON'T CARE WHAT YOU PLAY, YOU GET THEM IN
AND YOU GET THEM OUT! THAT'S AN ORDER!! 137

CLOSING 147
INDEX 149

ACKNOWLEDGEMENTS

For me to write this book was challenging enough. But how quickly did I find that the most challenging part was writing the acknowledgements, because, I didn't want to leave anyone out. But I soon realized that there is no way I could possibly mention everyone who has encouraged me over these past four years and not miss anyone. Therefore, to the many who have encouraged me during this time, THANK YOU so much from the bottom of my heart!

There are special acknowledgements I would like to make to a few people who I also consider to be the wind beneath my wings during the last four years.

First – I want to thank God for having faith in me to be the writer of this book and giving me the directions in which I should go, from giving me the title, chapter titles, chapter outlines, jokes, and on and on. Also for the many people that he put in my path, who encouraged me very strongly to write this book. I told them that I was not the type to write a book and that I couldn't see me doing this; however, they kept insisting. One day, I literally went into a closet, looked up, and asked, "God, are you trying to tell me something?" After this, so many things took place that let me know that I was to write this book.

To David Reid, Author of: *Leading to the Bedroom, The Christian Couple's Path to Greater Sexual Intimacy and Freedom.* David has been my mentor and very gracious of the giving of his time to guide me and help me with all of the steps in making this book a reality.

To Bill and Lottie Kershaw, what a great couple! They have practically seen me almost every day (Monday – Friday each week) for the last four years at the restaurant I work at. They were relentless in their encouragements and support by being an ear to listen and letting me share the many things that took place for this book to happen. They have unofficially adopted me as their own and have shown much love and kindness to me. Lottie never wanted to leave until I told her a joke, she loved my jokes – and Bill also! There were times I didn't have the time or didn't have a joke to tell; so she made me tell her two the next time they came in, which really kept me on my toes to be ready to share laugher at any given moment.

To Max and Brenda Holland, for their support and encouragements. Brenda was very supportive in proof reading the book and offering her knowledge and making correction and suggestions. Max and Brenda always wanted to hear a joke or two as well, and would love to share them with others. I really value our friendship that we have had together over the past four years and I am very thankful for having them as friends.

To Elisa Colvin, for her support and encouragements and also for proof reading the book. She told me that she liked it so much that she read it twice. Elisa shared with me how she really connected with several of the stories by thinking on how much it reminded her of her brothers. She shared with me how she could see them doing what I wrote about in the stories and that meant a whole lot to me, because, one of the several goals I had in mind for this book to accomplish was for people to be able to connect and think of fond memories of their lives as well. I told Elisa a story that had happened to me while in basic training and since then, she has over and over for the last 31/2 years requested that I add it to the book. So, in chapter twelve the story was added in dedication to her.

I in no doubt know that in my heart, Gloria Robinson, a co-worker, prayed many of prayers for me during this time. We all know that prayer is the gate way to God moving in our lives. A great big "God Bless You" to her for being a prayer warrior and for her continued encouragement over these past four years.

To Pastor Beverly Kempson, who have been such an encouragement to me and a prayer warrior as well. During the time of writing this book, Pastor Beverly gave me an opportunity to be a guest comedian at a banquet her church held to help raise funds to purchase a church van. That night really boosted my perseverance and confidence to continue to press on with the book and be ready for whatever doors may open in my future to spread humor. A great big God Bless You Pastor Beverly.

As strange as this may sound, I want to acknowledge me for: Listening to wisdom, taking council among many, receiving corrections, keeping a humble spirit, and remembering that if it wasn't for God and the many people that he put in my path, I would be nothing.

TO GOD BE THE GLORY!

FOREWORD

Humorist

A person who acts, speaks, or writes in a humorous way
A person with a good sense of humor.

Comedian

A professional entertainer who tells jokes or performs various other comic acts.

An actor in comedy.
A writer of comedy.
A person who amuses or tries to be amusing; a clown.

When thinking about myself I wonder: Am I a humorist or comedian. In looking at the two definitions I can see myself falling into each category, both humorist and comedian.

What would make me a comedian; after all I am not a professional entertainer. Now, on the other hand, I tell jokes, acted in local comedies, I have written comedy skits, I try to amuse people and many of my friends call me a clown.

So, what would make me a humorist? I have acted, spoke and wrote in humorous ways, and I have a good sense of humor. Do you notice that in the definition of a humorist there is no mention of being a professional? Therefore, I see myself as more of a humorist because I am one step off on being a professional.

Some of the criteria's for a professional include the following:

1. A professional is a person that is paid for what they do. Qualifications have little to do with being a professional as one of the world's "oldest professions" is strictly a monetary gain career. An amateur may be more qualified than a professional but they are not paid, thus they are an amateur.

2. Expert and specialized knowledge in field which one is practicing professionally.

3. Excellent manual/practical and literary skills in relation to profession. High quality work in (examples): creations, products, services, presentations, consultancy, primary/other research, administrative, marketing or other work endeavors.

4. Reasonable work morale and motivation. Having interest and desire to do a job well as holding positive attitude towards the profession are important elements in attaining a high level of professionalism.

5. Professional Attire – Including but not limited to, dress slacks, long-sleeve button down shirt, tie, dress shoes, etc.

In looking at myself, at the present time, amateur best fits who I am. I don't get paid for spreading humor or being a comedian. Therefore, if one or more of my family and friends love the way I tell jokes, write humorist stories, act funny and goofy and they leave laughing waiting for the next time we are together for more of the same, then I need to pass a hint to at least leave a dollar, that way I can then call myself a professional.

Now before you go any further reading this book, allow me to set a few perimeters:

I decided to write this book because of the urging and encouragement of several friends of whom I have had the privilege of knowing for quite some time now. While thinking of all of the reasons why not to write, many uncanny situations came about that led me to believe, I am suppose to do this. No matter what the outcome may be, I am confident that someone is going to pick this book up, read it, and laugh and maybe shed tears of laughter.

While writing this book I kept this in mind: I want to write the book just like I would be telling it to you in person, I believe this will make this book more personal. For example: Correctly I would write: Jack and I... - incorrectly I would write: me and Jack.... - But the second way is how I would say it to you in person.

It is a proven fact that if people would learn to laugh or remember to laugh they would have no reasons to go to the doctor as much. Many physical symptoms of pain, anxiety, and fear are simply caused by not laughing. When we laugh, healing agents that are in our bodies get busy and start chasing out the bad, negative agents which in turn cleanses us from a lot of impurities.

Not only does this apply to those who laugh, but it also applies to those who cry. Crying and laughing; the two major factors in our lives that will make a difference not only in our lives, but also to those around us.

It has been taught for many of years that men should not cry. Well, unlearn that! Man was also made to laugh, cry, and show emotion. Men, change your way of thinking. While our dad's got a lot of stuff right, the issue of crying or laughing was taught incorrectly. Personally, I believe it takes a man to laugh, cry and show emotions.

Sure, there will still be those who may poke fun, scorn or ridicule you, but take heart, there will be many who will hold you to the highest esteem for daring to be different and at the proper times, Laugh – Cry – and show Emotions!

During the preaching one Sunday, a member of the congregation had a heart attack and died. The call to 911 was made. When the emergency responders arrived they took out half the church members until they found the one who actually died.

Don't let this happen to you; don't be guilty of not laughing, crying or showing emotion so that you would be considered among the dead.

So, with that said; sit back with a snack, a glass of ice tea or a cup of coffee and be ready – because you are about to put a smile on your face and a song in your heart!

"In all of these years there is something about laughter that I have never thought of, which is: No matter what race, creed, color, sex, religion or national origin that you may be, all laughter sounds the same."* Gerald L. Cooper

*If this has been said before I know nothing about it, so, until I find out otherwise, it's my saying!

Chapter One

IT'S ONLY LAURIE!

I remember the first lesson that I had in picking up a girl who I invited to go on a church outing. I had to go to her door, get the girl, then open and shut doors for the girl and then walking the girl back to her door after returning her home.

I was approximately 9 or 10 years old living in Decatur, GA. I was very active with the youth program in my church. Back in those days our youth group consisted of those around 9 years old to about 32 years old.

Our youth director had announced that the youth were going to have a bonfire; wiener and marshmallow roast along with a hayride and games. We were told that we could bring a friend and the parents (of the younger ones) where assured that there would be plenty of chaperones for this outing just in case any of the boys decided to bring a friend of the female gender or vise versa. You must understand that at that age and considering where I lived we were careful not to say "girl friend" because several of us boys did not have our cootie shots yet and if we did have our cootie shots, for most of us boys even though we liked the girl she may not have liked us back. So, in light of these facts we always used first names and never the term, "a girl friend of mine." For a side note; sometimes us boys would stretch a little. By using their name we would say; "a friend of mine, who is a girl."

I decided that I was going to ask "a friend of mine, who is a girl" who lived two doors up from me, to the bonfire. I asked Laurie if she wanted to go and she asked her mother if she could go, then

Laurie's mother called my mother for the details and afterwards gave the approval for Laurie to go with me.

When the evening for the bonfire arrived I went running for the door shouting out, "Mama, I'm going to go get Laurie!" My mother said, Gerald, wait! We will pick her up. I replied, "Pick her up?" "She's only two doors up!" Still my mother said wait. Now that dumbfounded me. Laurie and I played together all the time and I knew she was perfectly capable of walking to our house to go to a bonfire. Never the less, I waited.

Well, we got in our car and went two driveways up and pulled in. When the car stopped I just sat there. My mother then gave me the instructions to get Laurie. I rolled the window down and hollered, "Laurie we're here!" My mother interrupted and said, "Gerald go to the door and get her." I replied, "Go to the door?! Can't you just blow the horn?" - "Gerald, go to the door and get Laurie" I quickly replied, "Yes ma'am'."

I was one bewildered little boy while walking to the door. When I got to the door I knocked on the door and of all things Laurie's mother opened it. I asked, "Is Laurie ready?" Her mother replied, "Here she is." "I quickly replied, "Come on!" I turned to go and by this time my mother had rolled down her window. She stuck her head out and said, "Gerald, ask her if she is ready to go." I stopped and said, "She's ready." My mother said, "Ask Laurie if she is ready." I looked at Laurie and asked, "Are you ready?" By then I was totally dumbfounded, after all it was only Laurie. Laurie replied, "Yes".

With relief I started for the car again and then I heard my mother say, "Gerald, wait and walk her to the car and open the door for her." My thoughts by now were that we weren't ever going to get to that bonfire. I never realized how complex taking a girl, (who is a friend), to a bonfire could be.

I then said, "Open the door for her, Laurie knows how to open a door!" Again my mother instructed, "Open the door for her." "Yes ma'am." I opened the door for her and when she got in I shut the door and went around the other side and got in, and off we went.

When we got back that evening, while driving up in Laurie's drive way my mother gave more instructions. I had to get out, go around, open the door, walk her to her door and make sure that she was in before I left.

(Laurie had told me at the outing that her mother had given her instructions to wait for us to come get her and wait for me to come to the door. I was to make sure that she was ready, walk her to the car, open the door and shut it for her. When we returned she was to wait for me to open her door and let me walk her to the door. Then, when she got in the house, I was to leave.)

So, when the car stopped, I got out, went around, opened Laurie's door, walked her to her door (unbeknownst to me, her mother had the door just slightly cracked opened). I looked at Laurie and asked, "Is this where we kiss now?"

Laurie's mother quickly opened the door and said, "Not this time! Laurie, tell Gerald good night." Laurie replied, "Good night, Gerald, thank you for taking me, I had a good time." Laurie went in and as I walked back to the car, I thought, well, it was worth the try, after all that I been through tonight, not only did I want that kiss, I deserved that Kiss.

JOKES

IT BETTER LINE UP WITH THE BIBLE

A young man was going to take a girl out for their first date. He escorted her to the car, opened her door and she got in, he shut the door and went around and got in. Before he could start the car the girl looked at him and very seriously and forcefully said: **WHAT EVER WE DO ON THIS DATE BETTER LINE UP WITH THE BIBLE!** *The young man very shocked at her actions and words replied: "OK!"*

Well he took her out to dinner because the Bible teaches: I was hungry and you fed me, then they went to a movie be-

cause of having the joy of the Lord. While sitting waiting on the movie to start, the young man looked over to the girl and asked; "Can I kiss you?" The girl looked at him and replied: **"ONLY IF IT LINES UP WITH THE BIBLE!"** The young man thinking, "Oh Brother! What did I get into?" After a few minutes of thinking, his face lit up, he leaned over to the girl and gives her the biggest kiss across the lips that one could ever give. This gave the girl a tremendous shock and she sat back and asked: **WHERE DOES THAT LINE UP WITH THE BIBLE?!"** The young man replied: "Matthew 7:12 – Do unto others as you would have them do to you!"

<u>SINNER, SINNER, DOWN BELOW</u>

A preacher's oldest son invited his girlfriend over after Sunday services for lunch.

Noticing that his son had a worried look on his face, the preacher took his son into the living room, sat on the sofa and asked him what was bothering him.

Unbeknown to them both, the youngest son slipped in behind them and hid behind the sofa listening to what was being said.

The oldest son said, "Dad, when we are finished eating, me and my girlfriend will probably go to the apple orchard and walk around. I also believe that we will sit down and after a little while we will want to kiss." "Dad, will it be alright for us to kiss?"

The preacher replied, "Son, whenever faced with a situation that you are unsure on what to do, just stop and pray; the Lord will direct you."

After lunch the boy asked his girlfriend if she would like to go to the apple orchard. Without his knowledge, his younger brother ran ahead and climbed up in one of the trees. The oldest son and his girlfriend walked around for a while and then sat under the very tree, that his younger brother was in.

The moment came when they wanted to kiss and the oldest son said: STOP, I MUST PRAY FIRST!" He then closed his eyes, turned his face toward the sky and prayed: "Lordy, Lordy, Up Above, Can I Kiss the One I Love?"

His younger brother looked down and replied: "Sinner, Sinner, Down Below, Pucker Up and Let her go!

BODY GUARDS

A girl who was waiting on her date was given a Bible to take with her. She asked why she should take along a Bible. Her dad replied: "If that boy starts to move to fast and wants to get to frisky, just put the Bible between you and him, because, he won't be able to crawl over Matthew, Mark, Luke and John!"

DATING PHILOSOPHY

FORSHAME FOR A COUPLE TO GO TO A DRIVE IN THEATRE THEN GO BACK HOME AND BE ABLE TO TELL WHAT THE MOVIE WAS ABOUT.

CAREFUL WHAT YOU PRAY FOR

OK, I must confess, I was dating a girl who was literally blind. Two months ago I made a mistake and took her to a faith healing service where she was prayed for and her blindness went away. She took one look at me and I haven't seen her since. :(:(:(:(:(:(:(

SHOULD HAVE HAD THAT LONG TALK

A young man called his mother and announced excitedly that he had just met the woman of his dreams and was wondering what should he do? His mother advised: "Send her flowers, and on the card invite her to your place for a home-cooked meal!" So that's what he did. His mother called the day after the big date to see how things had gone. "The evening was a disaster," he moaned. "Why, didn't she come over?" asked his mother. "Oh, she came over," he said, "But she refused to cook!"

FROM THE SINGLE GUY

Being single I needed some excitement, so over the past few months I have been going to Walmart for some fun.
Unfortunately, I didn't have anyone to go with me, so I came up with things to do on my own.
So, this is what I have been doing:

1. I took 24 jars of wrinkle cream and randomly put them in women's carts when they weren't looking.
2. I set all the alarm clocks in house wares to go off at 5-minute intervals.
3. I made a trail of ketchup on the floor leading to the first aid kits.
4. I walked up to an employee and told her in an official voice, "Code 3 in house wares. Get on it right away!" I really had fun watching her run around looking dumbfounded. I learned later that she was new and wasn't really sure what 'Code 3' was.
5. I went to the lay away department and tried to put a bag of M&Ms on layaway.
6. I placed a 'CAUTION - WET FLOOR' sign on a carpeted area.

7. I set up a tent in the camping department and told the children shoppers they could come in if they would bring pillows and blankets from the bedding department to which twenty children obliged.
8. When a clerk asked if they could help me I began crying and screamed, "Why can't you people just leave me alone?" EMTs were called.
9. I looked right into the security camera and used it as a mirror while I picked my nose.
10. While I was looking at the fish in the fish department, I decided to try out my new rod and reel.
11. I darted around the store suspiciously while loudly humming the 'Mission Impossible' theme.
12. In the auto department, I practiced my 'Madonna look' by using different sizes of funnels.
13. Several times I hid in clothing racks and when people browsed through them, I yelled "PICK ME! PICK ME!"
14. When an announcement came over the loud speaker, I assumed the fetal position and screamed "OH NO! IT'S THOSE VOICES AGAIN!"
15. I took a hand full of those reading glasses off the display and asked the clerk where the fitting room was?

And if that's not enough;

16. One night I went into a fitting room, shut the door, waited awhile, and then yelled very loudly, "Hey! There's no toilet paper in here."

One of the clerks passed out. I sure had fun!

CHECK UP

I just had a check up yesterday and now I'm going to have to do something I have been putting off for a long time. I'm going to have to get me a girlfriend - My Sugar Level is Low!

PURE BLONDE

I took a blonde out on a date. I took her to a mom and pop restaurant. When we walked in there were only 15 tables in the whole place. One of the walls was covered completely with a mirror so that it would give the impression that the restaurant was bigger. We sat down and ordered our food. While we were waiting, my date kept looking over to the mirrored wall and then said. "Gerald, there is a couple over there that looks exactly like us." I sat there and in my mind I was thinking, "Lord this is too good to pass up, but I'm going to mind my manners and not say anything." Well, we got our food and after a while of eating, my date slammed her fork down on the table and said, "That's it!" I asked, "What's wrong?"

She replied, "I'm going over there to meet them." All I knew to say was, "Go Ahead!" She got up and started to walk across and then she stopped, looked, and then turned around and came and sat back down. With sort of a "snickerish" type of laugh I asked, "What's Wrong?" My date said, "Oh nothing, she's coming over here!"

CHOOSE YOUR SONGS WISELY

I dated another blonde one time, and took her to a restaurant. After we had ordered, we begin to talk and get to know each other. I discovered that she was an Elvis Presley fan, so, I thought how romantic it would be to serenade her with an Elvis Presley song. I stated to sing, "Your Nothing but a Hound Dog,

Crying All the Time..." – She got up and left and I haven't seen her since.

TIME TO GO

After dating a girl for three weeks, I had to break it off. I found out that she was telling everyone that I was talking behind her back and pushing her around. So, what did she expect, she was in a wheel chair!

MIRANDA RIGHTS

(This is Miranda Rights for a man when a woman ask him to guess her age)

YOU HAVE THE RIGHT TO REMAIN SILENT,
WHATEVER YOU SAY
WILL SURLEY BE USED AGAINST YOU.

IF YOU GIVE UP YOUR RIGHTS, WHAT YOU SAY
WILL BE USED AGAINST YOU IN A COURT OF LAW
AS THE WOMAN JUSTIFIES
KNOCKING YOU UP SIDE YOUR HEAD,
SUCKER PUNCHING YOU,
FOLLOWED BY A SEVERE BODY SLAM.

YOU HAVE THE RIGHT TO AN ATTORNEY,
IF YOU CAN NOT AFFORD AN ATTORNEY,
TO BAD,
YOU SHOULD HAVE HAD THE SMARTS
TO REMAIN SILENT.

I TRULY HOPE YOU UNDERSTAND YOUR RIGHTS!

Chapter Two

SALSBERRY STEAK IN THE CAN

Years ago me and my older brother was going on a hiking trip on the Appalachian Trail starting at Clingmans Dome hiking to Siler's Bald and back. It was suppose to be just me and him. Well, without me knowing, my brother decided to bring along a young boy from his church who attended my brother's Wednesday night class. I didn't find this out until I got to my brothers apartment the night before we were to leave. I tried to be diplomatic by stressing to my brother that it was suppose to be just me and him. He said he understood but he had told Tony that he could go because his father didn't do much with him and that he also had told the his mother that he could go.

    Not wanting to cause any ill feelings, I agreed even though I was still apprehensive. We went to the store to get our food and one of the items my brother picked was this big heavy can of tomato soup. I asked him, "Who's going to carry that can?" He replied, "You are." I said, "No I'm not; let's get some lighter stuff because I ain't carrying that can." My brother said that he would carry it so in the cart it went.

    Well, we got the rest of our food items, which included more canned stuff, picked out by my brother, and we went back to his apartment, packed the rest of our back packs and went to bed so that we could be refreshed for the following day.

    I must stop and mention this. While at the store and the apartment, Tony was doing some mischievous things and I kept telling my brother, we didn't need that kind of behavior while hiking the Appalachian Trail because if he couldn't behave before the trip he could put himself and us in danger by not minding while up in the mountains. My brother tried to assure me that everything would be alright and not to worry, and that he would have a talk with him and make sure he would act right.

The next day we finally arrived at Clingmans Dome, got everything set and off we went. The mountains were just plain beautiful. Here we were hiking where there were no cars, telephones, nor pagers, only the magnificent beauty of creation.

Just so you will know, the distance between Clingmans Dome and Siler's Bald is approximately six miles. In my opinion, once we got to Siler's Bald it felt like it had been a twenty mile trip. However, before we would get to Siler's Bald we had an overnight stay, which was our first stop, at Double Springs Gap. This is where the story really gets interesting.

Upon arrival there was a lean-to there. A common name for the lean-to is adirondack shelter. It was a three sided shelter with a metal roof, the front had a chain link fence with a gate to keep little to medium size critters out and to slow down a bear, so if needed, you can make atonement to your maker before the uninvited bear came in.

Inside the adirondack was an upper and lower sleeping area. Logs were placed horizontally from the back of the adirondack to the middle, supported by other logs that were supported by more horizontal and vertical logs. Covering the horizontal logs was a wire type fencing stretched from one side to the other, layered two times.

On the trail you come across all sorts of people. Being that my brother and I were in our early twenty's, it appeared that the good Lord was smiling on us when we met two attractive girls about our same age there. Now before you freak out on me, all thoughts were honorable and hiking on the trail and sleeping in the Adirondacks are coed. Later that evening a husband and wife came up and slept the night as well, so there you are, chaperones.

As we got up to the adirondack, Tony saw that they were the only two girls there and us, so he decided to offer that we set up our tents and let the girls have the adirondack for themselves. I looked at him, thinking, Boy – shut up! Obviously you have not reached the point in life where this was an important – "thank you Lord moment!" I then looked at my brother with piercing eyes and he looked at me then looked at Tony and said, "Come on, let's go get some water!"

We went to the little creek and as my brother began to lecture Tony I poured all the water out of all our canteens and then filled them up again. Right when I was about to finished with the third canteen I told my brother and he concluded his lecture.

We went back to the adirondack and Tony spoke up again, "I still say we need to give the girls their privacy and"…..my brother interrupted him and said in a stern, firm voice; "Do you want to go get more water?" Tony quickly replied, "NO!"

After introductions, we went inside the adirondack and sat our backpacks down. Shortly thereafter, my brother and Tony went to gather some firewood.

Now let it be known, I can be sneaky and do things in a sly way that I know will get to my brother. No, I don't do it all the time but this is one of the times that I did. While they were gone I noticed that the girls had put their bedrolls on the upper right side of the adirondack. Well, guess where I put my bedroll? You guessed it! Right next to theirs! I also hung my backpack up with rope and a piece of cardboard off one of our boxes. I punched a hole in the middle and pulled the rope through it and put it middle ways down the rope to keep the mice from climbing down the rope and getting into my backpack. Just so you will know, mice will climb down a rope to get to a backpack, but with the large piece of cardboard on the rope mice will stop. They will not climb onto the cardboard because it would give way and they would fall to the ground. Even if the cardboard were hard, they would still stay off of it because they would not be able to hold on to the cardboard without falling. So, the little mice would then turn around and go away.

The two girls notice what I did and ask why I did it. After explaining how it worked they asked me if I would do theirs also. Great, my brother isn't here and I'm racking up the brownie points!

After taking care of their back packs, I got down, went and sat on a log that was on the inside next to the chain link fence, and began to whittle a point on the bottom of a walking stick that I had acquired along the way. One of the girls came and sat down next to me and began to hold conversation. On the outside I was calm and cool, just being little ole humble me – but on the inside my heart was racing a hundred miles an hour and I was thinking, "YES LORD!"

As we were talking a little mouse came out from under the lower level sleeping area and grabbed a crumb that it had spotted. The girl grabbed my right arm and said, "OH GOD!" I threw my walking stick with my left hand at the mouse and missed it by only inches and then the mouse turned and ran from whence it came. Still clinging to my arm she was shaking and saying how much she hates mice. I don't like mice neither, but on the inside I was praying as hard as I could, "LORD, SEND ANOTHER ONE!" I was thinking that if the Lord would send another mouse that girl would be in my lap!

Well, my brother and Tony made it back with some firewood and the girls went for a walk. While they were gone my brother told me that he was thinking that we would have the soup we brought with and another item. I believe the soup can got heavy for him while on the trail and that's why he decided on soup, so that he wouldn't have to carry it anymore!

Not long after the girls were gone I asked my brother if he noticed where the girls had their bedrolls. He looked up and saw where they had them, and then I said, "Do you see where I put my bedroll?" My brother looked at me and said, "Do you mean to tell me that I brought you all the way up here and this is the thanks I get?" I simply replied, "Yep!" He then said, move your stuff now! I replied, "Nope!" My brother was about to really get upset but saw that the girls were returning. To look good in the girl's eyes he stopped and let the issue pass.

Well, it was getting time to prepare for supper so my brother tried to start a fire in the fireplace but wasn't having much success. After a couple of attempts one of the girls offered to do it for him, but not to be outdone by a girl, he said that he could do it and besides he taught men and boys how to start fires. The girls asked what he meant and after explaining to her she went back to do what she was doing. After a few more attempts he looked at me and said, "I know what to do." So my brother went to his backpack and took some toilet paper off his roll turned around and saw where one of the girls had gone over to the fireplace and had a nice fire going. My brother looked at her and asked, "How did you do that?" She replied, "Experience."

I started to laugh and he turned and looked at me and said, "Hush!" As my brother was telling me to hush, I looked down and my eyes got big when I saw one of the girls pull two big steaks out of their cooler that was still wrapped in the cellophane.

My brother turned to see what had my attention and he asked the girls where they got the steaks. One of the girls explained that they often came out for the night and returned back the next morning and usually brought steaks to eat.

As I mentioned earlier, my brother ain't going to let no girl get the best of him if he can help it. So, not to be outdone, my brother turned to me and said, "Gerald, instead of eating what we were planning to eat (noticed it is now what WE were planning, where just a short time earlier it was him doing the solo planning), why don't we eat the STEAKS that we brought tonight?"

I looked at him and in a loud, sarcastic kind of voice replied, "OH, YOU MEAN THEM SALSBERRY STEAKS IN THE CAN!"

The girls couldn't hold it in any more, they began to laugh, and feeling outdone, my brother began to scold me and told me to stop all my little antics.

The night came on and still my brother was in his mode of trying to impress the girls, but that is another story for another time.

I will tell you this, I still threw in a few more innocent but sly antics because the girls kept telling me from time to time how cute and funny I was and it tickled them because they saw what I was doing as just having fun.

So, if you hear someone with a loud, sarcastic kind of voice saying, "Oh, you mean them salsberry steaks in the can!" It may be a good chance that's me!

JOKES

A LIFE-SAVER

A good piece of chocolate has about 200 calories. As I enjoy 2 servings per night, and a few more on weekends, I consume about 3,500 calories of chocolate in a week, which equals one pound of weight per week. Therefore, in the last 3-1/2 years, I have had chocolate caloric intake of about 180 pounds, and I only weigh 165 pounds. So... without chocolate, I would have wasted away to nothing about 3 months ago! I owe my life to chocolate!

WORTH BEING PICKY

A new supermarket opened near my house. It has an automatic water mister to keep the produce fresh. Just before it goes on, you hear the sound of distant thunder and the smell of fresh rain. When you pass the milk cases, you hear cows mooing and you experience the scent of fresh hay. In the meat department there is the aroma of charcoal grilled steaks with onions and mushrooms. When you approach the egg case, you hear hens cluck and cackle, and the air is filled with the pleasing aroma of bacon frying. The bread department features the tantalizing smell of fresh baked bread and cookies. But one thing is for certain, I don't buy toilet paper there anymore!

NO KIDDING!

A lady was picking through the frozen turkeys at the grocery store but she couldn't find one big enough for her family. She asked a stock boy, "Do these turkeys get any bigger?" The stock boy replied, "No ma'am, they're dead."

WHEN'S DINNER?

When I was growing up there were times when my mother was cooking that the smoke alarm went off. We would tease her by saying that was the dinner bell. When I got married my new bride was cooking and something set off the smoke alarm. Without thinking I just blurted out, "Time for dinner!" Needless to say that didn't set to well with her. As time passed, it became a part of our lives as well!

DEVILED HAM

While reading the Bible one night something occurred to me; Deviled Ham is mentioned in the Bible. Mark 5:12, 13 "...and the devils besought him, saying, send us into the swine" – "...and the unclean spirits went out, and entered into the swine....

FIRST FISH DINNER

For you fishermen: The first fish dinner is mentioned in Matthew 14: 13-21. Now-a-days, we add French fries, coleslaw, backed beans and the bread is called hush puppies!

THE OLD TIME CLASSIC

What do you call a cow lying on the ground? Ground Beef!

MIS-INTERPRETATION

A man went into a restaurant one night with an ostrich. The waiter came over and greeted the man and did a double take on the ostrich, and then proceeded to take the man's order. The man said, "I would like the salad tonight," and the ostrich replied, "And I'll have the same." When they had finished eating the bill was $7.26.

The man pulled out of his pocket the exact money and laid it on the table. The waiter thought to himself, now that's pretty impressive. The next night the man came in again with the ostrich and told the waiter that he would like to order the spaghetti dinner. The ostrich replied, "And I'll have the same." When they had finished eating the bill was $11.47. The man pulled out of his pocket the exact money and laid it on the table. The waiter thought to himself, that's really strange. The next night the man came in again with the ostrich and told the waiter that he would like to order the T-bone steak dinner, with a baked potato and all the trimmings. The ostrich replied, "And I'll have the same." When they had finished eating the bill was $37. 97. The man pulled out of his pocket the exact money and laid it on the table. The waiter then said, "Sir, now hold on. For the last three nights you come in, you had the exact money for what you ordered. How do you do that? Do you go home and study our menu on our website and then do the math, then come in with the exact money?" The man replied, "No." The waiter then asked, "Then how do you do that?" The man explained, "Well, I was cleaning out my garage and found an old dusty lamp. I wiped it off and out came a genie. The genie told me for setting him free I was going to be granted two wishes. So the first wish that I had was for, no matter what I wanted to buy in my life, I would always have the exact money for it." The waiter replied, "Wow, that's smart thinking!" The waiter then pointed toward the ostrich and asked, "What's with the ostrich?"

The man said, "Oh, my second wish was for a long-legged chick, covered with feathers, and would agree with everything that I had to say!"

WHAT'S THE DIFFERENCE

A man was ordering a pizza at his favorite pizza restaurant. The waiter asked, "Sir how would you like your pizza cut – 4 or 8 slices?" The man replied, "Better make it 4, I don't think I can eat 8!"

MORE INFORMATION PLEASE

A young man had a student that he had met in another country to come visit him in the United States. After a couple of weeks, the student asked him to teach him how to order in the diner. The young man said, "Sure" then said, "Let's start with something easy. Say, "Apple Pie and Coke." The student slurred his first try then the young man told the student, "Sound it out like this: A-p-p-l-e P-i-e and C-o-k-e." After the second attempt the student got it right. The next day the student went to the diner and sat at the counter. The cook came over and said, "Hi," and asked, "what will it be?" The student slurred his first attempt and the cook asked, "What?" The student, remembering how his friend told him to sound it out, said, "A-p-p-l-e P-i-e and C-o-k-e." The cook said, "Oh, OK" After about 6 weeks of the same thing, the student asked his friend to teach him how to order something different in the diner. The young man said, "Sure," and then said, "Say, Ham and cheese sandwich." The student slurred his first try and then the young man told the student, "Sound it out like this: Ham – and – Cheese – Sandwich."

After the second attempt the student got it right. The next day the student went to the diner and sat at the counter. The cook came over and said, "Hi" and then asked, "The usual?" The student shook his head no and then said in one fast big slur, "Hamandcheesesamwich." The cook asked, "WHAT?" The student, remembering how his friend told him to sound it out, said, "Ham-and-Cheese-Sandwich." The cook then asked, "White or Rye?" The student not knowing what to say repeated his order, "Ham-and-Cheese-Sandwich." The cook said, "Alright, white or rye?"

The student with a be-withered look on his face repeated his order again. "The cook with a frustrated voice said, "Alright, I know you want a ham and cheese sandwich, but, do you want white or rye?" The student, not understanding and not knowing what to answer, squinted his eyes and with a frustrated look said, "APPLE PIE AND COKE!"

EASY DIET

According to a recent article I just read on nutrition, it said eating right doesn't have to be complicated. Nutritionists say there is a simple way to tell if you're eating right. Fill your plates with bright colors; Greens, reds, and yellows. In fact, I did that this morning. I had an entire bowl of M&M's. It was delicious! I never knew eating right could be so easy. I now have a whole new outlook on life.

QUESTION

What disease did cured ham actually have?

Chapter Three

HERE COMES THE BEARS!

In chapter two I introduced the story about going to the Appalachian Trail with my brother and a boy named Tony. This story is another adventure we had while on that trip.

During the time on the trail, Tony had this nasty urge to get ahead of me and my brother. We were constantly telling him to stay with us and not get ahead. We tried to explain that it was not safe to get ahead by his self because he could get hurt or some wild animal could jump out and get him.

There was several times when Tony got ahead of us that we just said we'll catch up because he will get tired and sit and wait on us. At one point we heard Tony start to yell, "Bear! – Help! – Bear!" My brother and I began running to catch up with Tony just knowing that we were going to confront a bear. When we caught up with him, Tony would start laughing and telling how funny we looked running to catch up to him. Needless to say, we both scolded him and told him that what he was doing was not funny and was not a good joke to do on a trail, but, nevertheless, Tony kept doing it.

We finally got to Silers Bald and what a site! It was simply beautiful up in the mountains and we were having a great time in the wilderness. We were not supposed to stay the night at Silers Bald; however, my brother decided we would stay. I kept telling him that our permit called for us to stay the night at the next stop and not Silers Bald. I also noticed that the adirondack was quickly filling up and I just knew for sure that we were going to end up in a tent. I wasn't very happy with that idea knowing that a mother bear was somewhere up in those woods with her three cubs. An

Adirondack with a chain link fence will slow a bear down, but a tent was a whole different story.

Well, the night grew on and sure enough other campers were getting anxious about the room running out and some of them started to get out their permits to compare with everyone else to see who didn't belong there. To keep them from getting upset at us, I decided I would set up my tent. My brother went over to the campers and told them, not to worry, because I was setting up my tent. That calmed them down and the permits went back into the backpacks and all seemed well at the moment.

Soon, everyone was turning in and I went for my tent. I was really nervous about sleeping out in the tent, and also somewhat frustrated that not one time did my brother offer to stay in the tent instead of me, because, after all – it was him that caused this whole situation by not moving on to we were suppose to go – our final destination.

Now I did some advance planning for a line of defense in case some varmint or bear was to wonder into camp during the night. My first line of defense was my walking stick with the pointy end. My second line was my hand axe. My third line of defense was my knife. I didn't bother getting out of my pants and shirt figuring I may have to make a run for it, after all, [it is against the law to run in the mountains with a bare (bear) behind].

I did all that I could do to try to get to sleep but with no success. I did some cat napping but the naps only lasted about ten minutes at a time. As the night rolled on I was at the point of really falling asleep when I heard a voice coming from the Adirondack saying they believed that they heard a bear up on the ridge. It really made me nervous when one of the campers pointed a flash light up on the ridge and someone else said that they saw the bear as well.

It was then that I had great drops of sweat pouring off my face. I had one hand on my walking stick and the other hand on my hand axe. Just then I heard walking coming from the adirondack and I believe I would have qualified to be a human water fall. It felt like water flowing from my face and upper body more so than drops of sweat.

The walking got closer and then the bear called out my name. No! It was not a bear it was my brother. I breathed a sigh of relief. My brother asked me if I was OK and I told him, "Sure, I'm fine." (Liar, Liar, pants on fire)! He asked if I wanted to go into the adirondack and I replied that I thought it was full. He told me that there was one spot left on the bottom row and that it would not be difficult to bring my stuff in and get in that spot. I still, acting macho, replied, "I'm fine" but he still asked one more time if I was sure. I told him I was and then he turned and started back to the adirondack. In a low tone I shouted, "Hey, don't go away so fast, ask me one more time." My brother chuckled and turned around and asked if I wanted to go in the adirondack and I quickly replied, "Here grab this!" I had already collected my bed roll and was shoving it out of the tent into his hands.

I grabbed my back pack and went into the adirondack and after a few moments of adjustment I was snuggled in my sleeping bag ready to get some sleep.

I was just at the point of drifting off to sleep when I heard some strange noise and then someone with a flashlight started to shine it around the adirondack and then stopped on a mouse chewing on some toilet paper hanging from his back pack. He didn't hang his pack up right, so Mr. Mouse was helping himself to this guy's toilet paper. The camper got really ill and started to point his flashlight in my face accusing me of causing the situation. I very firmly but politely asked him to get the light out of my face and assured him I didn't cause the problem. Another camper then told him that he saw me hit his backpack causing the toilet paper to fall out and get hung up. I told them both that it was not me and when the second camper shined his light in my face he realized that I wasn't the one he saw. The second camper began to shine his light in everyone's face until he got to Tony he then replied; "Oh he's the guy, not the other one!" The two quickly apologized to me and the first camper by now had gotten up and ran the mouse off and resealed his toilet paper. By the way, when the two flashlights were shined in Tony's face he was sound asleep all of the commotion did not wake him up.

A new dawn had approached and everyone (except me, my brother and Tony) got up, cooked their breakfast, ate, cleaned up and then started out for their continued journey. Shortly thereafter, we got up, ate, cleaned up and were preparing for our return trip back to Clingmans Dome.

I didn't notice that Tony had drifted away from the adirondack. About the time I was looking around for him me and my brother heard the most blood curling scream for help that one could ever imagine. Tony was screaming, "Help! Bear! He's got me!" Total adrenaline went though me, I grabbed my walking stick and hand axe, ran out of the adirondack and started down the little hill where Tony was screaming. I thought for sure he was getting mauled. My brother reacted in a different way. Hurriedly, he came in the adirondack right as I was running out.

Now one thing I must tell you so that you can get the full picture of this; my brother had twisted his ankle (somewhat) and had sort of a limp. I turned to see if he was behind me yet and here came hopping on the good foot, holding up the bad foot while trying to aim his camera all at the same time! I yelled so as to be heard over Tony's yelling, "What are you going to do with that camera?" my brother replied, "I'm going to take pictures!" I replied, "TAKE PICTURES! ARE YOU NUTS?!"

Can you imagine this?

Brother – Oh this picture is where the bear was ripping Gerald's arm off...
This picture is where the bear had Gerald's neck in his mouth...
This picture is where the bear was pawing Gerald's leg putting big gashes in them....

Back to the story-
When we got close to the bottom of the hill, there Tony was on the ground laughing as hard as he could at the sight of me and my brother as we came charging down the hill to his rescue. I came

to a sliding stop as I realized that once again Tony was pulling another one of his "Help!" save me from this bear routine.

At that point I had reached my limit with this false alarm stuff. As I stood there deciding whether to give him the biggest butt whooping that he probably has ever had in his life, or drag him through those mountains myself until I saw a bear and throw Tony to the bear, I turned to my brother and said with the sternest voice that I knew to use, I said, "You had better talk to that boy and straighten him out, because the next time he hollers bear and there ain't no bear getting him, I'm going to handle it myself and he ain't going to like it!!!" I turned and went back up the hill to finish packing my back pack.

I don't know what my brother told Tony, but when they got back up the hill Tony came over and apologized to me and assured me that he would not do it again. I was still in a furious mode of thinking and I told him, "Tony I hear what you are saying and you had better mean it – because if you do holler bear again when one ain't attacking you, Tony, you ain't going to like me, and in fact you will wish it was a bear instead of me!" "Do you understand me?"

Very politely and meaningful from his heart he replied, "Yes sir." I stood and stared at him for a moment and then told him I forgive him, but don't do it again...and he didn't. In fact, from that time on, Tony was one of the most behaved, well mannered boy I ever have seen. Not one time did we have to get on to him or tell him to slow down and not get ahead.

I have always wondered what my brother told Tony and perhaps I will never know, but I do know this, Tony must have told everybody that I knew and even perfect strangers this story because I have never heard anyone yell in dire distress "BEAR!" ever again.

JOKES

BEAR BEHIND

A lady was jogging thru the woods in the mountains when suddenly she heard a noise. She looked behind her and saw a bear running after her. She quickly ran to the ranger station, ran inside the door, closed it and put the bar up. She turned and explained to the forest ranger what was going on. The forest ranger then arrested the lady. When she asked on what charges she was being arrested for, the forest ranger told her that it was against the law to run through the woods with a bare(bear) behind!

BATH TIME

I was camping with my brother one time, when during the night I was awoken by some noise. I looked at my brother and there was a skunk tapping my brother on his shoulder. My brother was sleeping on his back and opened his eyes and then the skunk looking down at him said, "Sir, I'm going to have to ask you to leave the area, you're ruining my reputation!

WINTER FOR TWO

A hunter was hunting for bear in the mountains and as he was walking down a trail, he did not notice a bear coming his way. When the bear got closer, all of a sudden the hunter and bear noticed each other. The hunter in great excitement raised his rifle to shoot, the bear raised up on his hind legs, and with both paws in the air said out loud, "DON'T SHOOT, LET'S NEGOTIATE!" The hunter in disbelief asked, "WHAT?" The bear said again, "DON'T SHOOT, LET'S NEGOTIATE!"

The hunter lowered his rifle and in somewhat disbelief that a bear was talking to him, the hunter said, "Alright, let's talk." Well, they sat down and the bear asked, "Just what are you looking for?" The hunter said, "Well, winter is coming on and I need a fur coat to keep warm." The bear replied, "Yes, I can understand that, you humans do need a coat for warmth." The hunter then asked the bear, "What are you looking for?" The bear replied, "Well, like you said, winter is coming on and I am about to go into hibernation so I need a full stomach." After some more negotiating, the hunter had his fur coat and the bear walked away with his full stomach!

WHEN ALL ELSE FAILS, PRAY

A man was hiking on a mountain trail when all of a sudden he heard a horrifying sound behind him. The man turned around and saw a bear running at him. The man began to run just as fast as he could, but soon realized that he would not be able to out run the bear so he dropped to his knees and began to pray, "Dear Lord, PLEASE LET THIS BE A CHRISTIAN BEAR!" All got silent behind him. The man opened his eyes and turn back to see if the bear was still there. There was the bear on his knees praying, "Lord, thank you for this I am about to receive...."

DON'T RUSH THINGS

A Pentecostal Minister, Catholic Priest and Rabbi would get together every month for a time of food and fellowship. One month while meeting, the Pentecostal Minister told the other two that he was up in the mountains last month and ran across a bear. After talking to the bear for a little while the bear gave his heart to Christ, and that he baptized the bear in the creek. The next month came and the Catholic Priest shared how he too had went to the mountains and he happen to run across the same bear that the Pentecostal Minister did the month earlier, and after talking to the bear for a little while, he had the bear taking communion. Another month had passed and the Pentecostal Minister and Catholic Priest showed up but the Rabbi did not. After a little inquiring they found out that the Rabbi was in the hospital in ICU. The Minister and Priest went to the hospital and upon arriving in the room where the Rabbi was they saw that his whole body was in a body cast from his neck down to his feet. The Minister asked, "Rabbi, what happened to you?" The Rabbi told the two that he was up in the mountains a few days ago and ran across the same bear that they did, and after a short while of talking, he came to the conclusion that the bear was not ready for circumcision!"

BUILDING TIME

Do you know how the Amish hunt deer? They find a deer and build a barn around it!

THE RIGHT DIRECTION

Two hikers were hiking along a mountain trail when they came to a fork in the trail. There was a sign that said bear right: So they went left.

SKUNK CHRUCH

Pastor Skunk was leading his congregation in worship when all of a sudden they heard a terrible noise in the back of the church. They all looked toward the door and there stood a big red fox and a bobcat. The skunk congregation began to panic but Pastor Skunk started to yell, "Don't panic, Let us Spray, Let us Spray!"

NEW SHOES

Roy Rodgers bought him a new pair of shoes. He put them on and then soaked them in a tub of water so that they would form to his feet. Afterwards, he put them on the back porch to dry. The next morning Roy Rodgers went to bring in his shoes and saw that they were gone. Close by Roy noticed cougar tracks. Roy set out on Trigger to get his shoes back. Later that evening, Roy returned with his new shoes and a dead cougar slung across his saddle. Dale met him as he rode up and seeing the dead cougar she asked with song, "Pardon me Roy, is that the cat who chewed your news shoes? (Sung as: Pardon Me Boys, is that the Chattanooga Choo Choo!)

FILL INS

A man was applying for a job at a zoo. The zoo keeper told him that his gorilla was sick and not on display, and he had several buses of people coming to especially see the gorilla. The zoo keeper asked him if he would be willing to put on a gorilla suit and go into the gorilla area and act like a gorilla while the tour was there. The man willingly accepted. When the tour groups came up to the gorilla area, he would do everything that he could to act like a gorilla. At one point he began to swing on the rope and without realizing it, he swung too far up and the rope snapped and he landed in the lion's area next door. Immediately the lion jumped on him and the man in the gorilla suit began to cry out with fear, shouting for someone to help him. Suddenly a voice came from the lion which said, "Quite man, or you will get us both fired!"

GOTTA KNOW THE SONG

What does a cow who has been milked 3 days late sing? "Saved to the Udder Most!"

LITERARY APPETITE

Two goats wandered into the junkyard and had a field day. One of them spent a particularly long time bent over a spool of film. When he was finished, the other goat came over. "So, did you enjoy the film?" The goat replied, "To tell you the truth, I liked the book better."

Chapter Four

I'LL WHOOP YOU IF YOU DO
and they said they would too!

Misunderstandings can happen very quickly especially when it involves two brothers and a friend.

I have been a member of a boys program for many of years. Through the years great memories have been made and it would take a set of novels to write about them all. But permit me to tell about a trip that happened back in my early years.

Our leader, Estel took about eight of us boys on a trip to the Okefenokee Swamp which is located in the southern part of Georgia. We had to take a side trip to pick up Commanders Estel's brother-in-law so that there would be two adults going. For some reason the other leaders of the church were unable to go. If memory serves me correctly, I believe Commander Estel's brother-in-laws name was John.

After picking up John, we continued on our journey until it got dark and Commander Estel pulled into a rest area where camping overnight was permitted. There were a lot of cars, trucks and several RV's as well. The rest area had the usual amenities which included several fire pit areas that resembled Bar-B-Q grills with chimneys. The pits were surrounded by pea gravel. (Those white little sized rocks).

We were told not to put up tents, we were just to lay our sleeping bags out and sleep on the ground with nothing in-between us and the sky. A few of the boys found them a spot close to our leader while Phil, his brother Bruce and myself laid our sleeping bags at the edge of one of the fire pits.

Before going to sleep, Commander Estel gave us instructions to go to sleep and no playing around. This was followed by a "yes sir" from all of us.

Well, I was laying there in my sleeping bag right at the point of falling to sleep – (ever wondered where the phase "falling to sleep" came from? After all, how does one "fall to sleep?") Oh well, back to the story.

Phil nudged me and I rose up and looked at him and asked, "What?" Phil pointed at a bat flying around and asked me if I wanted to see if we could hit him with those pea gravel rocks. I said, "No, I want to go to sleep." NOT! - I replied, "Sure!" So Phil and I began to throw rocks at the bat.

Now the direction in which we were throwing and the angle at which the rocks were coming down – kind of like an arch shape projection – the rocks were hitting a chain linked fence that bordered the rest area. Another bit of information you should know. If you were to draw a straight line from where Phil and I were and where the chain link fence was, my older brother was directly between us and the fence.

This is where it really gets good!

My brother was asleep in his sleeping bag and woke up to the sound of the rocks hitting the fence. He happened to sit up right as Phil and I tried to hit the bat again with the rocks hitting the fence. My brother didn't see the bat; he thought we were throwing rocks trying to hit him. Well, my brother found him some rocks and began throwing them at us. Knowing that my brother didn't know about the bat, I tried to tell him without waking up our leader that we weren't throwing at him. He didn't understand so he continued throwing at us, so we started throwing rocks at him, leaving the bat out of it. Instead of arch type throws, they became line drives.

At one point of the pea rock battle, my brother decided he wanted something bigger so he found some pine cones and began throwing them. Of course, we threw them back. Now if that ain't enough, one of those pine cones hit Bruce, Phil's brother, and woke him up and then Bruce got in on the action. Pine cones soon became sticks and Lord knows what all the other things we were throwing at each other. Anything we could get our hands on! As the battle progressed, Phil got his army style plastic canteen and began throwing it at my brother.

After the canteen made several trips back and forth, my brother paused for a moment and here came that canteen again. Only this time – my brother had unscrewed the cap and as the canteen came hurling through the air water was going all over the place. Needless to say, me and Phil got wet.

Ok, anything goes in war. Phil, Bruce and I got our canteens out, unscrewed the caps, and threw them at the same time at my brother and he got wet. My brother got smart. He kept our canteens and wouldn't throw them back. All that war got us thirsty and suddenly we were without water.

Out of the sleeping bags we came and charged my brother and we retrieved our canteens. Just as we laid back down our leader had gotten up and came over and seeing we were still awake instructed us to go to sleep. Whew! He didn't know about the war, he thought we were still awake talking. Commander Estel went back to sleep. The way we knew he was asleep was when he started that awful snoring.

There I was laying there in my sleeping bag almost at the point of falling asleep again when I heard a noise behind me. Somehow my brother had sneaked around us and started a fire in the fire pit where we were at. He then ran back around and got back in his sleeping bag hoping that our leader would get up and see it, and think that me and Phil did it. Phil and I got up, and having no water, we started to throw the pea gravel on the fire to put it out. Well, if that wasn't enough, my brother once again left his sleeping bag and began going from pit to pit, gathering up some pine straw, place it on the pit, light it and run. Phil and I would then go and put the other ones out.

Now I don't know why, but Bruce felt obligated to start going through the rest area knocking on peoples RV doors and then running. When I saw what Bruce was doing, I told Phil that we had better get back in our sleeping bags before someone came out and saw us thinking we were the ones knocking on the doors.

We got back in our sleeping bags and soon my brother started throwing things again. I decided that I wanted to go to sleep so I took my sleeping bag near our leader (but not to close because of the snoring) laid down and went to sleep. By now it was four o'clock in the morning.

Approximately eight o'clock, we were awaken by Commander Estel and his brother-in-law, John. After we got up, rolled up our sleeping bags and put them in the van, Commander Estel had all of us boys line up at a picnic table. He then pointed at a few of the boys and told them to stand next to him. Somehow or another he knew exactly which of us boys were in on the commotions during the night. He reminded us that his instructions were for us to go to sleep and no playing around but we decided to disobey.

He then took off his belt and had us turn around and bend over. Commander Estel and John gave us a "lick" with the belt. Commander Estel then told us if we disobeyed them again the same thing would happen, only with more licks. (Back then leaders did that with no thought of getting sued times sure have changed).

As we stood there rubbing our behinds' Bruce, crying, spoke to Commander Estel saying, "When I get back home I'm telling my daddy that you gave us a "lick" with a belt, and he's a deacon and he will have you thrown out of the church." You both are in a lot of trouble!" Bruce then said, "My daddy will tell their daddy's too and their dads will get you as well!"

When Bruce said that, something inside of me went into panic mode. Without really thinking, I stepped out of line, looked over at Bruce and said, "Bruce, if you go back home and tell my daddy or your daddy tells my daddy, I'm going to whoop you" and without hesitation the other boys said they would too! I in no way what-so-ever wanted my dad to find out that I disobeyed my leaders because I knew he would whip me good and I didn't want that to happen.

I looked at Commander Estel and John and told them that I was very sorry for disobeying and that I wouldn't disobey again. And, I didn't!

Needless to say, we slept until we got to a restaurant for breakfast, and then we slept until we got to Okefenokee Swamp.

In case you're wondering, Bruce never told his dad and Commander Estel or John didn't say anything neither.

Whew!

Another incident happened on the way back from Okefenokee Swamp - but that's another story for perhaps another book.

JOKES

BANK ROBBER

When I was younger I must confess that I robbed a bank. But the good side is, that I paid my brother back and bought him a new pig! I wasn't strong enough to break it with my hands, so I used my arm; they called it armed robbery!

SOUND SLEEPING

An Uncle who lived in the country invited his nephew who lived in the big city to come and visit him on his farm. The uncle's nephew had never been camping before and he wanted to take him. They found a place in an open field and set up their camp – tent and all. They cooked, ate, cleaned the dishes and sat back roasting marsh mellows and just had a grand ole time talking. Finally the time came for them to go to sleep, so in their tent they went and were soon asleep. Around two o'clock in the morning the uncle woke up the nephew and asked "look up and tell me what you see." The nephew replied, "I see the stars, the moon, the night sky and all its majesty. The uncle then asked, "What does that tell you?" The nephew said, "It tells me that we have a mighty big God, a mighty creator who formed and put all of this in place." The nephew then asked his uncle, "What does it tell you?" The uncle replied, "It tells me that while we were asleep someone came and stole our tent!"

THE CONSULTATION

"Doctor, I'd like you to evaluate my 13 year-old son." "OK: He's suffering from a transient psychosis with an intermittent rage disorder, punctuated by episodic radical mood swings, but his prognosis is good for full recovery." "How can you know all that without even meeting him?" "I thought you said he's 13?"

FACT OF LIFE

A boy, frustrated with all the rules he had to follow, asked his father, "Dad, how soon will I be old enough to do as I please?" The father answered immediately, "I just don't know, son. No male has ever lived that long yet."

E-MAIL FROM GOD

One day God was wondering how things on Earth were going so he called for one of his angels and sent the angel to Earth for a time to check things out. When he returned, he told God, "We have a problem on Earth; 95% are not living right and only 5% are living like they are suppose to." God thought for a moment and said, "Maybe I had better send down a second angel to get another opinion." So God called for another angel and sent him to Earth for a time. When the angel returned, he went to God and said, "Yes, it's true. 95% are not living right and only 5% are living like they are suppose to." God decided to e-mail the 5% that were good, because, he wanted to commend and encourage them for living right. Do you know what the e-mail said? "You don't?" OH, YOU DIDN'T GET ONE!!!!!!!

NEW INSIGHT

Two boys were walking home from Sunday school after hearing a sermon on the devil. One asked the other, "What do you think about all this devil stuff?" The other boy replied, 'Well, you know it's just like Santa Claus: It turns out to be your dad."

COMMANDMENTS

A Sunday school teacher was discussing the Ten Commandments with her five and six year olds. After explaining the commandment to 'Honor thy father and thy mother,' she asked, "Is there a commandment that teaches us how to treat our brothers and sisters?" Without missing a beat, one little boy answered, "Thou shall not kill!"

ROOM FOR IMPROVEMENT

An irritated father complained to his golf buddy, "When I was a kid, my parents sent me to my room without supper if I misbehaved. But my son has his own TV, telephone, computer, and every computer game and CD player in his room, so how do you handle it?" his friend asked. The father replied, "I would send him to my room!"

SIBLINGS

When my now 14-year-old daughter was three years old, her younger brother was getting into everything, she asked,

"Mommy, can we put him back, now?" Deciding to take this opportunity as a teachable moment in how siblings should treat each other, I explained to her that we could not put him back — that her brother was a gift from God. She looked up at me with her big blue eyes and responded, "I understand, Mommy. God didn't want him either."

GOLDEN RULE

Two brothers were in the back seat of the car on the way home from church. The older brother hit the younger brother several times, and so, the younger brother hit back and that's when the fight began. The father told the boys to stop and asked the younger boy why he hit his older brother. The younger brother replied, "I was just doing what the Golden Rule Says. He hit me first, so I thought that's what he wanted me to do to him!"

DON'T WASTE ENERGY

A little boy was sent upstairs to empty all of the trash cans. He came back down so quick that his mother asked, "So, how could you have emptied all of the trash cans that fast?" The little boy replied, "They didn't need emptying, just stepped in!"

WHO'S THE BLAME

There was a little boy who was standing on the cat's tail. His mother hearing the terrible commotion called from the next room: "Tommy, stop pulling that cat's tail!" Tommy said, "I'm just standing on it, he's the one that's doing the pulling!"

Chapter Five

πr^2 *(Pi – r^2)* {PIE ARE SQUARE}

For those who don't know what the title of this story is let me explain it before I get into the story.

π (sometimes written **pi**) is a mathematical constant that is the ratio of any Euclidean circle's circumference to its diameter. π is approximately equal to 3.14. Many formulae in mathematics, science, and engineering involve π, which makes it one of the most important mathematical constants. For instance, the area of a circle is equal to π times the square of the radius of the circle.

Needless to say there is a lot more to this than just this brief description. For all you mathematic geniuses, you know this from algebra.

When I was in high school, one of the required courses to learn in mathematics was algebra. Our semester on algebra started and about one month later our teacher left to pursue other interest. Our class was without an algebra teacher for about four or five months. Yes, I said four or five months. During this time there wasn't hardly anyone who ever came in as a substitute teacher, so, we found other things to do. Some caught up on home work assignments, others caught up on the latest gossip and if there wasn't any gossip (which was highly unlikely) they made some up, while others caught up on their sleep. Me and a friend were on the chess team so we played a whole lot of chess during those months.

Well, as fate would have it, the school leaders found out that one of the coaches in our sports department knew enough about algebra to come in and help us out, (Bless his heart)!

The first week of the coach being there, he got into the. Now the way I learn best is by relation. When that coach started to say, pie are squared I thought he was the biggest nut on earth. I just couldn't figure out where he was getting this "Pie are squared."

While sitting in my desk totally confused as one could be, the coach finished the lesson and announced: "If anyone would like some additional help, come stand in line." I was first in line. I literally ran to his desk. The coached looked up at me and asked, "OK, what do you need help with?" I replied, "Where do you get this "Pie are Squared" because, when my mother bakes a pie they are round!

The coach at first started to respond to me as if I was clowning around, but I remember him pausing and looking in my eyes. I truly believe he saw the sincerity in my asking the question and statement. The coach looked at all the other students who were in line and instructed them to go back to their seats because it was going to be a while with me.

The coach tried to explain that the "pi" he was talking about and my mother's "pies" were two completely different types of "pi's – pies." I still didn't get it so he sent me back to my seat and told me to just do the best I can.

Not long after that day another math teacher gave up her free period and came in and finished out the school year with our class.

When I got my report card I was really worried about what grade I had gotten in math. To this day I still don't know how I did it but somehow or another I made a "C" and passed!

Years later I took an algebra class and would you believe, I understood "pi" are squared" and did rather well!

Yep, in the world of algebra "pi's" are still squared and the precious memories of my mother's famous lemon margined pies and chocolate pies still linger. But most of all I remember that they were made to perfection and were always ROUND!

JOKES

YOU'RE CHEATS WILL FIND YOU OUT

I got caught cheating on a test in school. The way I got caught was my paper and my friends paper had the exact same answers wrote the same exact way, except for the last question. On the last question my friend answered, "I don't know." On my paper I wrote, "Me neither."

JUST A NOTE

The first graders were attending their first music lesson. The teacher was trying to begin at the beginning. She drew a musical staff on the blackboard and asked a little girl to come up and write a note on it. The little girl went to the blackboard, looked thoughtful for a minute and wrote, "Dear Aunt Emma, just a short note to tell you I'm fine."

HE KNOWS

"Take a pen and paper," the teachers said, "And write an essay with the title - If I Were a Millionaire." Everyone but Jimmy began to write; he just leaned back in his chair and folded his arms. "What's the matter, Jimmy?" the teacher asked. "Why don't you begin?" "I'm waiting for my secretary," he replied.

CREATION

A little girl asked her mother, "How did the human race appear, Mom?" The mother answered, "God made Adam and Eve and they had children, and those children grew and had children and eventually all mankind was made." Two days later the girl asked her father the same question. He answered, "Many years ago there were monkeys and apes from which the human race evolved." The confused girl returned to her mother and said, "Mom how is it possible that you told me the human race was created by God making Adam and Eve, and Dad said we developed from monkeys and apes?" The mother answered, "Well, dear, it's very simple; I told you about my side of the family and your father told you about his."

VERY PUNNY

Teaching high school English, Mr. Speller emphasized the importance of nice clean margins on student papers. One seventh-grade boy said in his essay that he was sorry to write in the margarine. When he graded his paper, Mr. Speller added a little note next to his that said, "Maybe next time you will do butter."

FLATTERY MIGHT NOT HURT

A teacher asked one of the students to give her a sentence with an object in it. The student said, "You're very pretty, teacher." The teacher asked the student, "What is the object?" The student replied, "A good grade in English!"

MAKING BABIES

Eight-year-old Susie came home from school and informed her mother that today in class they had learned how to make babies. The mother, rather shaken by the development, called the teacher to complain. After listening to the mother complain for a few minutes, the teacher responded, "Did you ask her to explain how it is done?" "No," said the mother. "Then ask her and call me back," replied the teacher. "So, how DO you make babies?" the mother asked her daughter. Susie responded, "You drop the 'y' and add 'ies'."

DONE WITH CLASS

One afternoon the young boy next door was cutting his grass, saw me and stopped and talked for a few minutes. He told me that cutting his grass was punishment for skipping a day of school. Then he asked me, "Why are you still doing your folks yard?" "Trying to keep a straight face I replied, "Because I also cut a class when I was your age." I'm told that he's had perfect attendance ever since.

DAD'S FLASH CARDS

After the Labor Day break was over, Johnny went back to school. The teacher asked Johnny if he had been working on his numbers, on how to count. Little Johnny said that he did and his father even helped him quite a bit. The teacher then said, "Alright, let see how much you know." What comes after two?" "Three" said Johnny. "What comes after four" asked the teacher. "Five" replied Johnny.

"What comes after six" asked the teacher. "Seven" said Johnny. "What comes after ten" asked the teacher. Johnny replied, "A Jack!"

SO YOU THINK

A college student went up to his professor after taking a test and said, "Professor, I must confess that I had help on my test. Before the test began, I prayed and asked God to help me, what shall I do?" The professor looked over the students test and then said, "Son, you have nothing to worry about, God did not help you on this test!"

FOOLED ME

I wasn't the brightest in class. When the teacher made me wear the dunce cap, she told me that I was an upside down snow cone. I believed her.

SO MUCH FOR EDUCATION

A hillbilly family was celebrating Junior's graduation from college. Junior is the only one in all of the generations up to now to ever go and complete all four years. There was singing, square dancing, laughing, eating, and all of the hootin' and hollerin' anyone can imagine. Paw got up and hollered, "STOP THE MUSIC, STOP THE MUSIC!" Then he said, "Junior, we are so proud of you so get up here and say some'um educated to us!" "Junior got up, straighten his bow tie, cleared his throat, and said, "Pi are squared" Paw hit Junior upside the head and said, "Junior, you know pies are round and cakes are square, now I sent you to college for four years, so, you had better say some'um educated or I am going to whoop you right here and now!"

Chapter Six

WE WEREN'T LOST; WE JUST WENT THE WRONG WAY

Every trip has its own unique story to tell. Sometimes the stories can be dull and the people who are hearing the story tellers' adventures could be thinking, "Who cares?"

Well, this is one of my many stories that I tell of a training trip that me and a friend named Dan went on. Our travels were to take us to Siler City, North Carolina and this particular trip would keep us away from home for over a week. Two trainings were being offered back to back so we decided to do both.

The training camps were held by a boys program with a national denominational church. The first camp was a staff school which would enable us to be training instructors for our national training camps which taught adult leaders class room teaching and camping skills. The second training camp taught survival techniques in the woods.

Dan and I have been leaders for a very long time. We taught all kinds of advancement merits to boys over those years which included how to read a map and compass. By the way, the maps included how to read road atlas maps as well as the road atlas maps in book form.

Dan and I were all set to go on our training journey. Just for fun I had put together an itinerary listing all the various towns that we would pass traveling along Georgia's I-85n starting from Douglasville, Georgia, to Siler City and approximate times in which we would be passing through. The approximate calculations of the travel time (including rest stops and supper) would be approximately six to eight hours.

Well, off we went. About an hour into our travels I started to notice signs along the way which said, "See Rock City." I thought to myself that it was strange to see those signs on I-85 north when Rock City was in Chattanooga, Tennessee. To get to Rock City you had to be traveling I-75 north.

Being so engulfed in our conversations I just brushed it off thinking they had put signs on I-85 as additional advertisement. Soon the signs became more and more abundant. At that point I just couldn't imagine why the tourist committee of Tennessee would go to great lengths to put so many signs about Rock City on I-85. Shortly after that thought, I saw a sign which read, "Chattanooga 8 miles." (I don't recall that exact miles on the sign but you get the idea)!

Just then I spoke up and asked, "Dan did that sign say Chattanooga? Dan replied, "I was about to ask the same thing." Dan also committed that he was wondering why so many "See Rock City" signs were along the way as well. I shared with him that I had been wondering the same thing. At that moment we both discovered that we were both thinking the same thing but neither one spoke up about it. Soon after there was this big sign announcing: Welcome to Tennessee! At that point we realized that we were traveling on I-75 north instead of I-85 north.

Well, we pulled off and had a good laugh. Yes, we laughed! Getting upset wasn't going to change the fact that we made a mistake. So, we pulled out a road map and after briefly looking at it we decided just to cut across the state instead of back tracking. You would think that we would have done the calculations on cutting across the state instead of back tracking but we didn't.

Going across the state through the mountains of Tennessee was our next mistake. We should have just backed tracked and we would have been better off.

Going through the mountains increased our fuel consumption and our travel time because of the winding roads, being behind logging trucks, older people who were not in a hurry for anything or anyone, and younger people driving slower because of being scared to death maneuvering the steep, winding mountain roads.

We took a supper break in Cherokee, North Carolina and called our spouses letting them know where we were. They were very confused on why we were in Cherokee instead of the point on I-85 we were striving for. After the explanation they too had a good laugh. We were also told that the extra gas money would be taken out of our allowances. LOL (Laugh out loud).

Dan and I took turns driving so that we could share in trying to get some sleep.

After a couple more stops for a stretch break and refueling, we finally made it to our destination. Our miscalculations added about two – three extra hours in travel time and extra fuel. There wasn't much difference in miles traveled but mountain travel and non mountain travel is two different things when it comes to time and fuel.

We arrived at the camp and after two hours of trying to sleep in the reclining seats in the car we got out, had a stretch and begin the day. By that night we were two leaders who were totally exhausted. After taking my shower and laying down on my bunk I was at the point of being asleep when suddenly I found out that the guy across the room was terrible with – SNORING!

JOKES

NO DONUTS?

Returning from a trip to visit my grandmother in California, I was stopped by a state trooper in Kansas for exceeding the speed limit. Grateful to have received a warning instead of a ticket, I gave him a small bag of my grandmother's delicious chocolate-chip cookies and proceeded on my way. Later, I was stopped by another trooper. "What have I done?" I asked. "Nothing," the trooper said, smiling. "I heard you were passing out great chocolate-chip cookies."

LAST WORD

A couple was riding in the country at odds with each other. They passed a field with a bunch of donkeys grazing. The man looked at his wife and asked, "Relatives of yours?" The woman replied, "Yes, by marriage."

PULLED OVER

"Hey you pull over!" shouted the traffic cop. The woman got a ticket for not making a complete stop at the stop sign. The next day the judged fined her twenty-five dollars. She went home in great anxiety lest her husband, who always examined her checkbook, should learn of the incident. Then inspiration struck and she marked the check stub, "One pullover - $25.00"

PULL OVER!

A blonde was driving down the highway while knitting. A state trooper got up beside her and saw that her window was down so he yelled to her, "Pull Over!"
The blonde shouted back, "NO, sweater!"

UGLIEST WOMAN

Two rednecks went to South Georgia to find them a pig so as to bring back for a BBQ. They found one running loose along the highway and after a short chase they cornered the pig, got out of their truck and caught it. They put the pig in the front of the truck with them and then headed back home. About five minutes after heading back home they were pulled over by two State Troopers. By the time the two Troopers had made their way to both sides of the truck, the passenger had put a hat on the pig. The trooper on the driver's side looked in the window and then asked, "What's your name boy?" The driver said, "Charlie Brown." The Trooper said, "Huh, Huh." Then the trooper looked at the passenger and asked, "What's your name boy?" The passenger said, "Peter Pan." The Trooper said, "Huh, Huh." Then the trooper looked at the pig and said, "Who's that in the middle?" The driver said, "That's my wife." Just then the passenger nudged the pig and the pig went, "OINK!" The Trooper then told the boys to go on and not get into any trouble.

When the Troopers got back in their car, the one Trooper looked at his partner and said, "You know, that Oink Brown is the ugliest woman I have ever seen!"

HEARING LOSS

A man was driving down the highway when he got pulled over by a state trooper.

The driver asked the trooper if he was speeding and the trooper said, "No, but do you know that a woman fell out of the back right door about three miles back?" The driver replied, "Oh thank the Lord, that's my mother-in-law, I thought I had lost my hearing!"

GOTTA LOVE IT!

A man was driving down the highway and got pulled over for speeding. The trooper asked for the man's driver's license and insurance card. While the man was pulling them out of his wallet the trooper happened to look in the back seat of the car and saw three penguins. The trooper exclaimed, "Sir, what are you doing with those penguins? You're not supposed to be carrying penguins in your car. When I get finished writing this ticket, you take them penguins to the zoo!" The man said yes sir and left after getting the ticket. The very next day, the same highway, same location, the same time, the same trooper pulled him over for speeding again. The trooper told him that he was going to give him another ticket for speeding and while waiting for the man's license and insurance card, the trooper happened to look in the back seat of the car and there sat those same three penguins but this time they were dressed in Hawaii shirts. The trooper said, "I thought I told you yesterday to take those penguins to the zoo!" The man replied, "You did, and they loved it so much, today we are going to the beach!"

MAKES YOU WONDER

Men are notorious for getting lost while driving and not stopping and asking for directions. Makes you wonder; was the GPS invented by a woman so women could get to where they are going without getting lost and at the same time protecting themselves from male pride? And have you noticed that most (if not all) GPS have a woman's voice!

PUNCTUATION

Two men were traveling when they stopped at a small town for lunch. They went into a local restaurant, ordered their food and sat down. While they were waiting, the two men got into a friendly debate on the correct punctuation of the town they were at. Soon the worker arrived with their order and one of the men decided to ask the worker if he would settle the debate on how to correctly pronounce where they were at. The worker agreed and said, "B-U-R-G-E-R- K-I-N-G!"

NO THANKS

A traveling salesman was ready for lunch so he stopped at a diner. Just before he got out of his car he noticed a sign in the window of the restaurant. The salesman started his car, pulled out and left. The sign in the window said, "Home Cooked Meals!" The salesman didn't want to eat there because his wife wasn't a good cook!"

HOME SWEET HOME

A man traveling back home stopped in a small town and stayed overnight in a hotel. The next morning the man went into the small town restaurant for breakfast. The waitress came over and asked, "May I take your order?" The man replied, "Yes, mess up your hair, take off your shoes, wrinkle up your apron, give me three eggs -awful runny, two slices of burnt toast, thick – hard to eat grits, and stale cold coffee, I'm home sick!"

MUST BE A REDNECK PROFESSOR

A professor traveling back to his college stopped at a connivance store. At the checkout, he looked at a particular item and asked the clerk, "What's that?"

The clerk said, "It's a thermos." The professor asked, "What does it do?" The clerk said, "It keeps hot things hot and cold things cold." The professor looked at it again and asked, "How does it do that?" The clerk said, "I don't know." The professor bought one and continued on his travels. The next morning the professor had the thermos sitting on his desk. A student walked in and seeing the thermos, he went up to the professor and asked, "Professor, what's that?" The professor said, "It is called a thermos." The student asked, "What does it do?" The *professor said, "I was told that it keeps hot things hot and cold things cold." The student looked at it again and then asked, "How does it do that?" The professor said, "I don't know." The student looked at the top and then asked, "What do you have in it?" The professor said, "Two cups of coffee and a popsicle."*

Chapter Seven

STEVEN: THE ONE THEY STONED BACK TO LIFE

A lot of strange things take place at church. You never know whom or what you might come in contact with. Let's re-word that. You never know what strange person you're going to meet next.

Let me set up this story for you.

I was in the Army stationed at Fort Bragg, North Carolina. Fort Bragg is located right outside of Fayetteville, North Carolina. I attended a church off post which is called Northwood Temple, Rev. Hedgepath, was (and still is) the Senior Pastor. When Pastor Hedgepath became the Senior Pastor, there were around 100 members in a moderate size church. In 1975 they had built a new building which sat 775 people. In 1985 they finished building a new sanctuary that seats 2,500. This story takes place in the sanctuary that was built in 1975.

One Sunday night after an evening service was over, my friend Rick came and found me in the sanctuary and said, "Gerald, come out in the foyer, I have someone I want you to meet." I said, "Sure" and off I went with him.

When I walked into the foyer I couldn't help but notice a man standing off to the side and it only took a few seconds of time for me to realize that there was something mighty strange about this person.

There was this strange person wearing – a long white rob – had long sandy colored hair just past his shoulders and a beard to match – wearing sandals – holding a long straight staff.

Without thinking I quickly looked at Rick and while pointing at the strange person I asked, "Is he Moses?" Rick told me to behave and said, "No, but ask him his name." I looked at who I thought to be Moses and asked, "What's your name?" Using a real sophisticated King James Version type of voice he replied, "I am Steven – the one they stoned back to life." I looked at Rick again and without thinking I said, "He's stoned alright!" Rick told me to behave and told me to ask Steven (the one they stoned back to life) what that meant.

Very nervously I looked at Steven (the one they stoned back to life) and asked, "What does that mean?" Again with that same sophisticated KJV voice he replied, "I was once a sinner on the way to a sinner's hell when I was saved by the stones thrown at me from the Word of God." I looked and Rick and said, "HUH!" Rick providing the translation said, "He was once a sinner but people witness to him and he gave his Heart to Christ."

I said, "OH." Rick then told me to ask him where he lived. Again, nervously I asked, "Where do you live?" Steven replied, "I live on the mountain top overlooking the valley of the shadow of death." (KJV voice). Again, I looked at Rick for the translation and Rick replied, "He lives in the house at the top of the hill overlooking Hay Street."

Now, for a little bit of explanation. Hay Street (at that time) was the "red light" district in Fayetteville, NC. That was the place for drugs, alcohol and mostly sinful entertainment which I won't spell out so that I can keep this book in proper order. I will also mention that it is to my understanding that all of that was cleaned up and the area is no longer considered the "red light" district.

On with the story.

After talking for a few minutes more, Rick asked me if I was going to Pizza Hut. After evening services, usually there were several of us young people who would go to Pizza Hut which was located about a quarter of a mile down from the church. They had a great salad bar in which most of us, if not all of us, would get. Then we had some fantastic fellowship. I said I was planning on it and Rick said that he was too. For some reason we were the only two that was going that night. Then it got interesting. Rick asked

Steven (the one they stoned back to life) if he would like to go and explained to him that everyone paid their own way. Steven in his KJV voice said, "Yes, I will splurge and go and partake of God's bountiful supply which came from his mighty creation." I then turned and looked at Rick, looked back a Steven and then looked at Rick again and asked, "Is that a yes?" Rick told me to behave and then said that it was a yes.

Rick told Steven to get to Pizza Hut, turn left out of the church parking lot and it will be about a quarter of a mile on the left. Folks; it gets even more interesting. I got out of my car, Rick got out of his, and Stephen got out of his carrying his staff. I looked at Steven and then his staff. Steven caught my eye looking and then said, "I guess it would be a good idea to leave this in the car." Rick and I both replied that it would be best. So back in the car went the staff and we went in and got a table.

While sitting there, Steven was looking at the menu and the waitress came and greeted me and Rick. She said, "Hi, how ya'll doing? Let me get your drink orders. She looked at me and I replied, "Sweet Tea." Rick did the same and when she looked at Steven - that is when she did a double take on just who was sitting in the chair. Rick introduced Steven to her and she said it was nice to meet him and then asked what he would like to drink. Steven replied: "I would like some Holy water." (Same KJV voice). She was looking down at her pad and started to write and repeat to him what he had said, – Holy waaaa... – and then quickly looked back at Steven and asked, "HOLY WHAT?" Rick very quickly told her to just bring the boy a picture of water and a glass.

Well, the waitress brought our drinks to us and then asked to take our order. Rick and I told her that we were going to have the salad bar and then she looked at Steven. The waitress asked, "Would you like the salad bar also sir?" (She had nervousness in her voice – wonder why) Anyhow, Stephen replied, "Yes, I believe that I shall partake of God's bountiful supply from the gardens of His majestic creation." She looked at me for help but I was staring at this guy with my jaw dropped down to the floor, stunned at Steven's answer. Realizing she was staring at me for help, all I could do was shrug my shoulders in bewilderment. Rick quickly spoke up and answered, "He'll have the salad bar." The waitress very quickly left the table.

We got up and got our salads and sat back down. Of all the things Rick could have done - he done went and did the other, Rick asked; "Who would like to bless the food?" Rick could have said, "I'll pray over the food" or "Gerald, would you like to bless the food" – NO – he had to ask who would like to pray. Steven said, "I would be honored to bless the food and thank God for this food we are about to partake."

We bowed our heads and Steven started to pray. He started out in Genesis, Exodus, Leviticus, and Deuteronomy, he continued with Joshua, Judges and Ruth. He hit a little 1 Samuel and 2 Samuel and jumped over to Ezra and Nehemiah. Then Steven prayed some of Psalms and Proverbs. If that wasn't enough, Steven then went on to the New Testament: Matthew, Mark, Luke and John and a little bit of Acts. He prayed out of a few more books and then concluded by saying, "And nourish this food to our bodies, Amen."

I have to admit, I didn't have my eyes shut the whole time. I kept staring at Steven and my salad while he prayed. When Steven got finished they started to eat. I just kept sitting there staring at my salad. Rick looked at me and asked, "Gerald, are you going to eat?" I replied, "NO!" Rick asked, "Why not?" I replied, "I'm too scared to touch mine!" Rick kicked me under the table and told me to behave and eat, and so I did.

Allow me to give you a word of wisdom. After your church service has concluded and one of your friends come to you and say that there is someone you need to meet in the foyer and you go with him and there stands a strange person wearing – a long white rob – has long sandy colored hair just past his shoulders and a beard to match – wearing sandals – holding a long straight staff, invite him to pizza hut. Tell him to turn left out of the church parking lot and when he is out of sight, you turn right and don't look back!

JOKES

WHAT YOU SAY CAN BE USED AGAINST YOU

President George Bush was walking through an Airport when he looked over and saw a strange person wearing – a long white rob – had long sandy colored hair just past his shoulders and a beard to match – wearing sandals – holding a long straight staff. President Bush said, "That looks like Moses, I want to go find out." So President Bush went over and asked, "Sir, are you Moses?" The man would not look him in the eyes and kept looking around. Again, President Bush asked the man, "Sir, are you Moses?" Again, President Bush got the same response. A secret service agent came over and said, "Mr. President we need to get you to your plane." President Bush said, "I know, but I have to find out if this man is Moses or not." The agent told President Bush that they would find out and to go on to his plane. After President Bush walked away, the agent asked, "Sir, are you Moses?" The man looked all around and behind him and then looked back at the agent and said, "Yes."

The agent then asked, "Then why didn't you tell President Bush that when he asked you?" The man replied, "Look, the last time I talked to a bush, I spent forty years wondering in the wildness!"

MIXED MESSAGE

I heard a story recently about a young girl who wrote a letter to a missionary to let him know that her class had been praying for him. But evidently she'd been told not to request a response to her letter because the missionaries were very busy. So the missionary got a kick out of her letter. It said, "Dear Mr. Missionary, we are praying for you, but we are not expecting an answer."

A CHANGE OF HEART

After Sunday school two little boys were standing in the church lobby. As they were talking, a pretty little girl from their class walked by them. One of the little boys said to the other, "When I quit hating girls, she's the first one I'm going to quit hating."

MORE PLAY ON WORDS

I have been wondering, if the tray liner that restaurants put on your tray to place your food on would to fall into the ocean, would it then be called an Ocean Liner?

DOUBLE MEANINGS

The National Chess competition had completed for the evening and all of the chess players went out for dinner. The chess player from Australia got everyone laughing after he was finished eating. When he was ready to go, he looked over at the waiter and said, "Check Mate!"

YA'LL COME EAT

I'm going to open two new restaurants. The first one is going to be a Country Western theme and instead of having a mechanical bull I'm going to have a mechanical pig. I'm going to call that restaurant - Bunking Ham Palace! My other restaurant is going to be a mixture between Italian and Soul Food. I'm going to call that one - YO, Mamma!"

ORDER PLEASE

A blonde went up to a lady at the desk and in a loud voice said, "I would like a hamburger, large fry and a Coke." The lady at the desk looked up and replied, "Young lady, this is a library." The blonde said, "Oh, excuse me," then whispering she said, "I would like a hamburger, large fry and a Coke."

CLOSE FRIENDSHIP

Three ladies were celebrating their 50th birthday together, so they went to their favorite restaurant because the waiters where real good looking. When they turned 60, they went to their favorite restaurant because the food was good. When they turned 70, they went to their favorite restaurant because they had good handicap parking. When they turned 80, they went to their favorite restaurant for the first time.

ALL VOTES COUNT

A young preacher had taken over the duties as the Senior Pastor in the local church. His dad who had just retired as a full time preacher continued to attend the church that he had started. Every time the young preacher started to give the sermon, his father would fall asleep and begin to snore. After many times of talking to his dad about not doing that, the dad just kept on falling asleep and snoring. One Sunday, the young preacher had a plan for when his dad would fall asleep and began snoring. Sure enough, the young preacher began preaching with a moderate to loud voice and noticed that his dad had fallen to sleep and was snoring. The young preacher stopped what he was saying and with a very soft voice he said, "Anyone who wants to go to hell..." then he shouted, "STAND UP!" Upon shouting stand up, the young preacher's dad woke up and stood up. His dad looked around and then said, "Preacher, I don't know what we are voting on, but it looks like, me and you are the only ones for it!"

VERY CREEPY

One day in the middle of the night, two dead boys got up to fight. Back to back they faced each other, drew their swords and shot each other. A deaf policeman heard the noise, and came to arrest the two dead boys. If you don't believe my story is true, asks the blind man – He Saw It Too!

DO YOU BELIEVE

It was the Sunday for the monthly baptism service. The creek was almost to the top of its banks because of some previous rains and couldn't be used, so the preacher had a large galvanized wash tub outside the church filled with water. People would come up and the preacher would ask, "Do you believe?" Each person would respond yes and then the preacher would dunk their heads in the wash tubs. The last man came up and the preacher asked, "Sir, do you believe?" The man replied, "Nope." The preacher dunked the man in the tub anyways. After the man came back up, the preacher asked, "Do you believe?" The man still said no. After doing this three more times, the preacher asked, "Sir, do you believe?" This time the man said, "Yes, I believe!" The preacher then said, "Brother, go tell it on the mountain top!" The man went to the top of the hill and yelled, "I believe that nut is trying to drown me!"

NAT KING COLE

A new single preacher arrived in town and decided to go out and meet the people. While walking down the side walk, two men came up to him and said, "Hey, you're Nat King Cole!" The preacher replied, "No, I'm the new preacher." All morning long people would look at him and say, "Hey, you're Nat King Cole," and he would give the same response, "No, I'm the new preacher." Later that afternoon the preacher started to visit houses outside of town. He went to one house, knocked on the door and the most beautiful women he had ever seen answered the door. She was wearing a black stunning sun dress and was looking mighty fine. When she saw the preacher she said, "Hey, you're Nat King Cole!" The preacher looked to his right and left to see if anyone was around, and then looked backed at her, and with song sung, "Rambling Rose..."

Chapter Eight

WHO SAID I LIKED LASAGNA?

In my early youthful life I didn't care for lasagna at all. I saw some pictures of something (in which I will not describe) that turned me off from eating lasagna. I managed very well in avoiding eating it for several years.

In chapter seven I told you about a friend of mine, Rick, who put me in the path of Moses: oops, excuse me, Steven – (the one they stoned back to life). Rick and I meet at church not long after I started to attend there. After a short time I had meet many of the younger adults there, one of them whose name is Pam. Pam, Rick, me and few others hung out together quite often.

I don't remember what lead up to this, but Rick somehow or another got in his mind that I liked lasagna. He told me that Pam made really good lasagna and that it was some of the best he had ever eaten. Being polite, I just smiled and nodded my head in agreement even though I had never had it, nor did I care to have it.

On one occasion Rick came up to me and said, "Gerald, I have a surprise for you." I asked, "What?" Rick said that he had talked to Pam and told her that I liked lasagna and I haven't had any in a very long time so Rick suggested that we have a lasagna dinner for the gang and that I would be guest of honor. Pam quickly agreed to host the dinner, (and if memory serves me correctly) we all would help with the expense of the food. But anyhow, the dinner was on.

After Rick told me that I tried all I could to not show the panic that was inside of me. What I should have done is tell him thanks, but no thanks, I don't like lasagna. The reason I didn't say anything was because I didn't want to hurt anyone's feelings, especially Rick's and Pam's.

I think it was about two weeks before the dinner was to take place and during those two weeks I was wondering how I was going to get out of eating that nasty looking lasagna. Well as fate would have it I never could come up with a good excuse and then the night of the dinner came.

We all meet at Pam's house and the misery was prolonged. Pam was running late that day and the lasagna wasn't ready. I thought that my way of getting out of eating lasagna was if she hasn't started it yet I was going to very quickly suggest we all go out to eat – MY TREAT!

But Rick once again intervened and the clarification was, the lasagna wasn't finished cooking.

RATS!

After some great fellowship, Pam made the announcement that everything was ready and come to the table. The salad, bread and the dreaded lasagna was served. I saw that I had no choice but to eat the lasagna.

Under my breath I prayed and asked God to give me special grace to be able to eat the lasagna, not for my sake necessarily, but for Rick and especially Pam's sake. Pam was bubbling with happiness and excitement that all of us was there and I did not want to be the one to burst her bubble.

I passed up praying insisting that someone else pray because I did not want to thank God for the lasagna. Yes, thank God for the salad and bread and of course the sweet tea and the great friends at the table, but not for that lasagna.

The salad was served – the bread was served – and then came the dreaded lasagna. Of course being the gentleman that I am I took only a small, and I mean small portion and started to pass the dish and once again Rick intervened, "DIG IN COOP, THERE'S PLENTY!" Pam looked at my plate and said, "Don't be shy there is plenty for all." So with no further delay, I got some more.

I stalled as long as I could. Ate some salad, ate some bread and drank some tea and now the moment I have been dreading has come upon me.

I took a bite and began to eat. I thought, not bad. I then took a bigger bite – that's not bad. Before you know it I was eating that lasagna like it was going out of style. The lasagna that Pam had made was terrific! I ate and ate hoping that I wasn't making a pig out of myself. Needless to say we all devoured that lasagna and I lead the way!

From that day forward I never dreaded eating lasagna again. May I say - I never had lasagna any anywhere else that could come close to Pam's lasagna. My mouth is watering now thinking about it.

As time went by I had to begin to watch out for foods with a lot of onions. My stomach and onions don't get along very good now. So, when I am looking for lasagna for dinner, I have to be careful of the onions and sodium level.

Here's my problem, it's a long way to Pam's house now and I can't just jump in the car and go get some of her lasagna. So I have to settle for what is in the store. We found each other on face book and we've been keeping up with each other from time to time. One night while talking on the phone with her, the conversation came up about that dinner. Pam laughed and said that she never knew that I didn't like lasagna. We had a great time of reminiscing those days.

Please do me a favor. If we are talking and I tell you that I don't like a certain food, don't tell Rick. He may get in his head that I do like it and the next thing you know he's done planned a dinner and that dinner might not end up as well as the lasagna dinner.

JOKES

THE EDUCATED ONE

My busy mother sometimes accidentally left pots and pans on the stove with the burners on, so she resorted to posting this reminder on the kitchen door: "STOVE?" My sister, back from college, noticed Mother's sign. Beneath it she taped her reply: "No — Door! Trust me. I went to college."

INNER PEACE

I think I have found inner peace. I read an article that said the way to achieve inner peace is to finish things I had started. Today I finished two bags of potato chips, a chocolate pie and a small box of candy. I feel better already.

CONFUCIOUS SAY...

Man who eats many prunes get good run for money.

LEFTOVERS

The minister's wife was a wonder at conserving food and rarely had to throw away a bit of it. At one meal she gave her husband nothing but leftovers that he viewed with great disdain. He began to pick at the food, causing his wife to say, "Dear, you forgot the blessing." He replied, "Listen, sweetheart, unless you can show me one item that hasn't been blessed at least two times, I can't see what another prayer can do for it."

HONEY, I'LL COOK

A man was trying to surprise his wife by doing the cooking. She took over when she found out that her husband thought that the water in a can of corn was – corn syrup.

FIRST TURKEY

I was asked to get a turkey for the Thanksgiving dinner. I found a turkey and shot it. I scared the mess out of everyone in the store.

GOING BY DIRECTIONS

A blonde had all of the animal crackers spread out on the kitchen table. Her husband walked in and asked, "What are you doing dear?" The blonde responded by saying, "Going by direction." Her husband asked, "What directions dear?" The blonde responded by saying, "The ones on the box." "And what does the direction say dear?" The blonde said, "Don't eat if the SEAL has been broken, and I'm trying to find the seal."

LITTLE ONES DO HEAR AND TELL

A little boy was asked to say grace over the meal. The little boy didn't know what to pray so he said, "Lord, I don't know what to say so I will say the prayer my Grandpa says before everyone gets here; Lord, let these people eat fast and leave quick, so that I can go back to my nap – Amen."

JUST A PINCH WILL DO

A man was celebrating his 100th birthday when one of his grandsons came to him and asked: "Grandpa, what is the secret of living to be 100?" Grandpa replied, "Every morning when you start to eat your oatmeal, put just a pinch of gun powder on it and you will live to see 100." Well, Grandpa soon died and left behind; 12 children, 24 grand children, 12 great grand children and a 30 foot crater at the crematory when they cremated him.

TIMES HAVE CHANGED

Growing up I remember that spam only came in a can. Now-a-days, it is also in a computers email.

REMEMBERING THE SONG

Jesus came and had dinner with me. After we ate we went into the living room to talk and have coffee. I asked him, "Lord, what would you like in your coffee?" "...and Jesus whispered Sweet and Low...!"

WHERE CAN I FIND IT

Jelly is a food found in jars - on bread - on children - and on piano keys, only to name a few.

Chapter Nine

DON'T FORGET THE HOTDOG!

America's Food - The Hot Dog.
Americans have a fascination with the hot dog. Everywhere you go there is someone who always claims to have the best hot dog and the best way to prepare and eat it.

The name hot dog dates back to the 17th century when a sausage maker referred to his sausage as a "little dachshunds" or little dogs. The name evolved from there.

Hot dogs are popular among Americans because they are easy to make, inexpensive, and most of the time delicious. Hot dogs can be prepared in a number of great ways such as - nuke-em - grill-em - sauté-em - roast-em - fry-em or boil-em. (Just a Note: For those not accustom to southern talk, "em" on the end of a word is short for - them)."

There are many toppings that can enhance the flavor of your hot dog. Some of the most common toppings used on hot dogs include ketchup, mustard, onions, relish, chili, cheese and sauerkraut.

Did you know that July is National Hot Dog Month, or that the average American eats 60 hot dogs a year (according to this, I'm not average, I eat way less than that), and in 1893, hot dogs became the standard cuisine for baseball games. Another interested trivia is that for years hot dogs came in packs of eight and the hot dog buns came in packs of six. I never understood the bread companies doing that until I learned about making money. You were forced to buy two packs of hot dog buns otherwise someone would be without a bun.

On with the story –

Over the years I have noticed that people would put their hot dog into the hot dog bun and then add their favorite toppings on top of it. That was alright for those who just used the standard ketchup, mustard and onions. Well, when it came to putting on the chili, cheese and other toppings, it became a sloppy mess once they began to eat it. I too did the same thing and had the same problem.

So, I got to thinking. How can I fix my hot dog so that I wouldn't have such a mess once I began to eat? Another lesson about southern talking: When southern people are talking about cooking we usually say we are going to go "fix" supper, or I'm going to "fix" me a sandwich. It's not the type of "fix" as if something is broke, the interpretation in this case is "fix" means to prepare or cook. Such as: I'm going to cook supper, or, I'm going to prepare me a sandwich.

On with the story –

So, many years ago I started to fix my hot dog backwards. I would put my toppings in the bun first. Even when I was eating it with chili, I put the chili in the bun along with the other toppings and then I would put my hot dog on top of it all. I found that I had solved most of the problem of having my hot dog and fix'ins fall all over my shirt. For the most part all of my toppings stayed in the bun with very little dripping.

After I started doing this I found that I had to tweak it a little bit more. Once I had all of my toppings in the bun, I then pushed the hot dog on the top to help compact everything. Needles to say, this caused my bun to split on the bottom and everything fell on the table. That created quite a mess. So I got me another bun and this time I just placed the hot dog on top instead of pushing it down on the toppings and all was well.

The tweaking didn't stop there. I was fixing me a hot dog one time and I got a bun, opened it and in the process of opening it a small split in the bottom of the bun occurred. Well I thought that it wouldn't hurt anything so I fixed my hot dog and when I started to eat it the split didn't hold up under the pressure of taking a bite of the hot dog. Needless to say, everything fell into the tray I had it in. Again, that created a mess. So I got me another bun and this time

I made sure that the bottom did not have a split in it after opening the bun and then I proceeded in fixing my hot dog again.

For the most part, I have been quite successful in eating my hot dogs without everything spilling out on me, the table or without other complications.

Well, there is that one exception.

I was traveling home one night, kind of tired and I stopped at a national chain service station and went inside for a little stretch. After taking a restroom break I looked over and saw the hot dogs. I got me a fountain drink, went over and fixed me a hot dog in the way that I have already described, went to the counter and paid for it, got in my car and off I went.

About a eighth of a mile down the road I reached for my hot dog took a bite and noticed something strange. I didn't taste the hot dog. Being tired I really didn't think to look; I just figured I had put the hot dog on the bun too far over. Well, I took another bite and still no taste of a hot dog. This time I looked down and behold no hot dog. In the process of fixing my hot dog I have forgot to put the hot dog on after the toppings.

I could not believe it! I thought for a moment that I would turn around and go back to claim my hot dog but I didn't because who would ever believe my story. I know I would have been skeptical if someone came in telling me that story, so on I went leaving the hotdog behind.

That experience taught me to tweak my fixing a hot dog even more:

DON'T FORGET THE HOT DOG!

JOKES

SHARING

I confronted our 3-year-old granddaughter, "Are you eating your little sister's grapes?" I asked. "No," she innocently replied, "I'm helping her share!"

GOD'S WILL

A lady was riding down the road and knew that the light on the donut shop would soon be on advertising that they had fresh hot donuts. She prayed and told the Lord that if it was His will for her to have fresh hot donuts, the parking spot at the front door would be available. She said that after six times around the block, it became His will!"

BE CAREFUL WHAT YOU WISH FOR

A farmer was out walking on his land one day when he spotted an object on the ground. He picked it up, brushed it off, and out came a genie. The genie told the farmer, "For setting me free, I will grant you three wishes." The farmer's first wish was for his 100 acre land to be turned into the most beautiful land that man has ever seen. "POOF" the land was turned into the most beautiful place that man has ever seen. It had many gardens, waterfall, tennis court, swimming pool, and the plushest grass that you could ever imagine. The farmer's second wish was for his house to be turned into the most elegant mansion ever seen by man. The farmer described each room in the mansion and all of the furnishings. In 50 of the rooms, the farmer wanted all of the wealth of money that they could possibly hold. "POOF" it was done as the farmer wished. The farmer couldn't think of anything else at the time, so the genie told the farmer that whenever he was ready, just make the wish and it would happen. The farmer spent the next couple of hours walking around his new land, and then he went to the mansion and went through all of the rooms, looking at all of its splendor. The farmer then sat down in his brand new recliner to watch some TV on his brand new, 72" plasma, satellite TV screen, with his dog on his lap.

After a while, the farmer went outside to look at some more of the gardens and to walk the dog. While doing so, a commercial kept coming back to him, so the farmer begin to sing the commercial's jingle, "O I wish I were an Oscar Meyer wiener...."

"POOF!"

THE CLASSIC CHICKEN JOKE - REVISED

There are three reasons why the chicken crossed the road.

1. To get to the other side.
2. To prove to the possum that it can be done.
3. They were building a chicken restaurant on his side and he didn't want to become a sandwich!

ECHO CANYON

I went on a hike with three friends. When we got to a certain area, one of my friends told us that the area was known as echo canyon. My friend gave an illustration. He went up to the edge of the canyon and yelled his name, "John!" The echo came back: John-John-John. My second friend yelled out his name, "Ralph!" The echo came back: Ralph-Ralph-Ralph. My third friend did the same but instead of using his name he said baloney. Then it was my turn, I went up and yelled out my name, "Gerald." The echo came back: Baloney, Baloney, Baloney!

DON'T MAKE SENSE

It don't make sense to me when people get upset at the owners of restaurants for killing and using dogs for their meat, then get a lawyer and sue the owners, and then after they win their case in court, the owners are forced to closed their restaurant. Then the people light up the old grill and celebrate by cooking hamburgers and hotDOGS!

NEW SALAD FOR THE MENU

"I would like to announce that next week we are going to have a new salad on our menu. It is called the 'Honeymoon Salad.' - LETTUCE ALONE!"

I WONDER

When we buy wieners we call them hotdogs even though they are cold. When we get ready to cook them, we say, "Get the hotdogs," even though they are cold coming from the fridge. When we cook them, we call them hotdogs and this time they are hot. But, after they sit out awhile, they get cold again and we still call them hotdogs. Since they are not hot all the time, wouldn't it make sense to maybe call them cold dogs or cold puppies before and after they are cooked?

CLOSED SUNDAY

I was put on a register last Friday where I work to see how I would do, it only lasted 3 minutes. A lady came up to me and asked, "Gerald, can I get a cookie sundae?" I said, "No, you have to get it today or tomorrow, we are closed Sundays! They put me back in the dining room.

ORIGIN OF A DESERT

Back in the old west there was a cook that rode along on cattle drives that was very famous for his cooking. The cowboys really loved the little short cakes that he would make for desert and so they gave him the nickname, Short Cake. During one of the cattle drives the cowboys came across an Indian tribe that became very friendly to them. Short Cake met an Indian squaw and decided to quit the cattle drive, marry the squaw and live with her in her village. Years had passed and Short Cake had became very ill. While the squaw was visiting another village, Short Cake died. The squaw was sent for. Days had passed and the squaw had not come back so the chief decided to go ahead and bury Short Cake in the white man's ways. Just as the Indian braves were about to lower Short Cake into the grave, the squaw came riding into the village, on a horse in full run, shouting, "Wait! Squaw bury Short Cake, Squaw bury Short Cake! And from this story we got our desert, Strawberry Shortcake!

HILLBILLY HOTDOG

Ingredients of a Hillbilly Hotdog are as follows:

Road kill, Possum Inners, Distilled White Lighting, Pickled Pigs feet, Hog Jowls, Crawdad legs, Bat wings, Used chewing tobacco (To preserve the flavoring), wrapped in a long sour dough bun.

BAD TURKEY

A lady wanted to buy a parrot from a sailor who was very reluctant to sell it to her. The sailor told her that he had taught the parrot some bad language and it would not be the best pet for her. After several times of insisting that she wanted the parrot the sailor sold it to her. The lady took the parrot home. The lady showed the parrot his new cage and the parrot cussed her because he didn't like it. The lady told the parrot that since this was his first time at the house she would over look what he just did. The parrot then cussed her again for what she said. The lady being patient told the parrot that if he continued to cuss she would have to discipline him. The parrot then cussed her for that. The lady immediately took the parrot and put him in the freezer. An hour later the lady opened the freezer door and asked the parrot if he was done cussing. The parrot with ice all over him and shivering with cold told the lady that he had seen the light and would change his language because his cussing days were over. The lady warned him that she would put him back if he did not keep his word. The parrot assured he lady again that he had changed his ways, but then asked the lady. "Can I ask you a question?" The lady said, "Sure." The parrot then asked, "What did the turkey do wrong?"

Chapter Ten

HAND PRINT ON THE FACE

You can't be too careful about what movies you go to see in theaters. Movies that look good could turn out to be real bummers. You have to be careful of the movie ratings as well. Unless you really understand what the ratings mean, you could find yourself in an awkward situation.

Most people when they are dating usually do the same old ritual of going out to eat and seeing a movie.

I remember a date I had one time many years ago that almost cost me my eyesight.

We decided to go see a movie that had come out and the rating was PG.

Now let's review. The following is what movie ratings mean in general.

G – GENERAL AUDIENCES – All Ages Are Admitted

Nothing that would offend parents for children by viewing.

PG – PARENTAL GUIDANCE SUGGESTED – Some Material May Not Be Suitable for Children

Parents urged to give "Parental Guidance." May contain some material parents might not like for their young children.

PG-13 – PARENTS STRONGLY CAUTIONED – Some Material May Be Inappropriate for Children Under 13

Parents urged to be cautious. Some material may be inappropriate for pre-teenagers.

R – RESTRICTED – Under 17 Requires Accompanying Parent or Adult Guardian

Contains some adult material. Parents are urged to learn more about film before taking their young children with them.

NC-17 – No One 17 and Under Admitted

Clearly Adult. Children are not admitted.

Now I must admit that we didn't think this particular movie would have any questionable scenes but not so.

There we were, sitting in the theatre on the very back row, middle ways of the isle. The movie was nearing the end when all of a sudden, just in a few seconds of time a naked women comes dancing across the screen and off again. It happened very fast, and caught most people off guard.

Well my date was quickly embarrassed and she did not want me to see this particular scene. In an effort to shield my eyes, her right hand came across her body with such great force that at the moment of impact on my eyes I saw stars, a great loud slapping noise was heard throughout the theatre, and I had a tremendous stinging pain across my eyes. Right before the moment of impact on my eyes the scene was over but her memento was not.

My date immediately apologized for doing that and believe it or not, I did not get mad. In the meantime people were turning around to see what all the slapping noise was about.

Now imagine, you're sitting in a theatre and you hear a great slapping sound - you're going to look to see what it was. As you are looking, a man is holding his face and his date is removing her hand but you don't hear her saying she was sorry, all you see is her mouth moving and her hand retracting. WHAT WOULD YOU THINK?

Shortly after the movie was over we begin to exit the theatre. As we were walking through the foyer to the outside door I was still feeling my face because of a little stinging that was still there. People were looking at me and whispering to one another that I was the guy in the back of the theatre that got slapped. I'm sure they were thinking that I said or did something inappropriate and she stopped me.

All along my date kept looking at me and apologizing. Once we were in the car I turned on the interior lights and looked in the mirror – and there it was - one gigantic imprint of a right hand on my face covering the eyes. The impact was so hard that the imprint was still there and that is what my date and all the other people were looking at as we left the building.

Still, believe it or not, I didn't get angry or mad; I just looked at my date and said – "OUCH!"

Well, I guess there is good out of everything. From that experience I got a new nick name from her. From then on I was known as her – Raccoon.

JOKES

HELPING A STRANGER

Two guys were in Walmart looking around while pushing their shopping carts not watching where they were going. As they rounded the end of the isle on opposite sides of each other they hit their carts head on. They quickly apologized to each other. One of the men spoke up and said that he was looking for his girl friend. He said that she gets into Walmart and seems to get lost, and so, without looking where he was going, he collided his cart. The second man said that he was doing the same thing. The first man asked the second man what his girlfriend looked like." The second man said, "She is about 5'9, weights approximately 125 pounds, has long flowing red hair, baby blue eyes, the perfect nose, ruby red lips" and continued to describe a fine figure of a women. He then asked the first man what his girl friend looked like. The first man said, "FORGET MINE! LET'S GO FIND YOURS!

ADVICE TO AN OLD GUY

An old guy was working out in the gym when he spotted an attractive young lady. He asked a nearby trainer, "What machine should I use to impress that lady over there?" The trainer looked him up and down and said, "I would try the ATM in the lobby."

MOTHER TO THE RESUCE

A young girl who was engaged to be married came to her mother very upset. She said, "Mother, you know how much I love John and how much I want to marry him, but I just found out that he does not believe in Heaven or hell, what shall I do?"
Her mother replied, "Honey, you just keep being your sweet, innocent self and you will convince him of Heaven, and I will take care of the other side!"

IMPRESSING THE YOUNGER ONES

A lady was wanting to impress a younger man on her first date by doing a face lift, going to a tanning bed, working out at a gym and buying new style of cloths. The night had finally come when they were out on their first date. After sitting in the car kissing for a while the lady ask the younger man if he felt that she looked like she was forty. The younger man trying to be nice replied, "I'm sure at one time you use too!"

REDNECK CULTURE

A lady convinced her husband to take her to the opera. The man did not like the idea much, but, he went anyway. On the first act the man leaned to his wife and said, "That opera feller is a farmer." The wife asked, "How do you know?" The man replied, "Because listen to what he is saying he's saying: Vigoro – Vigoro – Vigoroooo." His wife asked, "So, what does that prove?" The man replied, "Honey, everyone knows that vigoro is a fertilizer!

RICE PREFERENCE

A young woman really thought she was being very patient through a long period of dating with no talk of marriage. One night her boyfriend took her to a Chinese restaurant. As he was looking at the menu, he asked her, "So, how do you like your rice? Steamed or fried?" Without missing a beat, she looked over her menu at him and replied clearly, "Thrown!"

IN AND ON, WHAT'S THE DIFFERENCE

A professor of an acting class had all of us students somewhat confused when he was trying to encourage us to pursue an acting career. He told us, "If you successfully complete this course, you will have a great chance of being in a movie or on TV." I asked the professor, "Sir, why do you say in the movies or on TV, what's the difference?"

CAREFUL WHO'S CALLING

A man went home one night and went into the kitchen to kiss his wife hello. As he walked in, she hit him upside his head with a 12" cast iron skillet. It laid him out on the floor. When he woke up, he sat up and asked, "What was that all about?" His wife said, "I was cleaning today and I found this slip of paper in your drawer with the name Linda on it." The man replied, "Honey, I bet on horse races, and that's the name of the horse I was betting on!" His wife said, "Oh honey, I didn't think about that, can you ever forgive me?" The man said that he forgave her and all was well.

The next night when the man came home, he once again went into the kitchen to kiss his wife hello and she hit him upside his head with a 12" cast iron skillet. It laid him out on the floor. When he woke up, he sat up and asked, "Honey! What was that all about?" His wife then replied, "YOUR HORSE CALLED TODAY!"

NOT BY CHOICE

A billionaire in Texas invited many of his friends to his house for a party. During the party, the billionaire took his friends to a very large swimming pool. What was so unusual about the pool was that it had about 30 alligators in it. The Billionaire told his friends that if anyone was brave enough to swim across the pool and get out on the other side; he would give them 25 million dollars. At first no one took him up on his offer, when suddenly a man went into the pool with a great splash. The man frantically swam to the other side and got out. The billionaire told the man, "I really didn't think anyone would do that, however, I am a man of my word." So the billionaire gave a check for 25 million dollars to the man. Then the billionaire asked, "Well, what is the first thing that you are going to do with your new found fortune?" The man replied, "I'm going to buy a ball bat, because I am going to knock the crap out of the person who pushed me in that pool!"

AMISH COW

An Amish farmer was milking his cow early one morning. When the bucket was half full, the cow kicked the bucket over. The Amish farmer walked to the front of the cow and said,

"Cow, Thou Shalt Not Kick Over the Milk Bucket." *The farmer returned to his stool and began to milk the cow again. When the bucket was half full, the cow kicked over the bucket again. The Amish farmer walked to the front of the cow and said, "Cow, Thou Shalt Not Kick Over the Milk Bucket," then he returned to his stool and started over. When the bucket was half full, the cow kicked the bucket over again. The Amish farmer went to the front of the cow and looked it straight in his eyes and said, "Cow, Thou knowest that I cannot smiteth thee, however, if you kick that milk bucket over one more time, I am going to sell you to the Baptist man on the other side of the street and he will beat the mess out of you!"*

MECHANIC OR EMERGENCY ROOM

I was playing baseball with some friends a week ago. One of my friends, who was an Indian, was pitching for the other team. My friend threw the ball and I swung so fast that I missed ball and the bat came out of my hand and went swinging through the air and hit him on his forehead. The hit was so hard it sent him to the ground. We all rushed over to help him. I saw where his head was cut opened by the bat and was bleeding pretty bad. I said, "We need to get him to a hospital really fast!" One of my other friends looked at me and said, "I can help him." I looked at him and said, "No you can't, you're a mechanic!" My friend said, "That's right, I went to college for four years to learn how to be a mechanic and they taught us how to fix all kinds of engines!" (Think about it)

GEORGIA WOMEN

Three men were sitting together bragging about how they had set their new wives straight on their duties. The first man had married a woman from Pennsylvania. He bragged that he had told his wife that she was going to do all the dishes and house cleaning. He said that it took a couple of weeks, but now he comes home to a clean house and all of the dishes are washed and put away. The second man married a woman from Ohio. He bragged that he given his wife orders that she was to do all of the cleaning of the dishes, do all the cooking, and clean the house. He said that after the first week he saw little results. After the second week she had improved tremendously. By the third week, he came home to a clean house, all the dishes were cleaned, and supper was ready and on the table. The third man married a girl from Georgia. He boasted that he told her his house was to be cleaned, dishes and laundry washed, and the cooking done, all when he got home. He said for the next three days he didn't see anything, but, by the fourth day some of the swelling had gone down and he could see a little out of his left eye. GOTTA LOVE THOSE GEORGIA WOMEN!

Chapter Eleven

THAT'S MY DADDY!

For over forty seven years I have been involved in a boys program with my church. The program provided Christ like character formation and servant leadership development for boys and young men in a highly relational and fun environment.

After getting out of the Army and getting involved in my local church I became a leader over several churches. I had the responsibility of promoting the program which, at that time, included about eighteen churches in the western/central part of Georgia.

I was also involved with a group of people who did frontier camping.

Each person chose a persona and an outfit of his choosing. I chose Indian Beadwork and I have a Buckskin outfit with a coonskin hat, complete with eyes and tail.

I made it a point to personally visit each church that was involved in the program at least twice a year and visit churches that wanted to start the program in their church. From time to time my wife would go with me along with our two girls.

I had a pastor contact me about coming to his church and presenting the program to his congregation. Chuck, a leader who was involved in the program went with me to the church to help. On this occasion, my wife and girls went along with us because the church was close by. At this particular time my oldest daughter, Elizabeth, was six years old and my youngest daughter, Rebecca who we called Becca, was three years old.

We arrived to the church early to meet with the pastor. The plan was for me and Chuck to stand in the foyer and upon our introduction we would come from the back to the pulpit and begin our presentation. I was dressed in my uniform and Chuck was in his frontier outfit.

My wife had taken the girls inside the sanctuary and was seated on the right side facing the pulpit. The church was not a big church. It was small and the sanctuary held around one hundred people at the most.

Soon the pastor got up and began to share with the congregation that he wanted to start the boys program in the church and had invited us to come speak. He then introduced us by name and we began to walk down the center isle of the sanctuary.

As Chuck and I were walking toward the front, Becca jumped up in the pew and began shouting and waving: "That's my daddy! Hey daddy! I'm over here daddy!" Becca looked down at her mom and said, "Look, there's daddy!" My wife with a horrified look on her face was trying all she could to quiet Becca, but to no avail. Elizabeth started to giggle and all that my wife knew to do was to grab her purse and things, Becca, and head for the back door telling Elizabeth to follow her. As they headed for the back door, Becca continued shouting. "Bye daddy! Mommy's carrying me out; I guess I'm too loud!"

While all of this was happening, I was looking over and smiling still heading for the pulpit.

As Chuck and I got up to the platform we greeted the pastor who was smiling and laughing, and then we turned around as my wife and daughters were just about to go through the back doors with Becca still shouting, "Bye daddy, I'll see you later, I love you daddy!" By then the doors were closed and you could still hear Becca say; "That was my daddy!" Shortly, the excitement of the shouting from Becca had stopped. People in the congregation was laughing and smiling from ear to ear.

There I stood not knowing what to say. I looked at Chuck as in saying with my eyes, "What do I do now?" Chuck was a great help. All he did was look at me smiling and laughing with the rest of them shrugging his shoulders."

I then looked back at the pastor and then to the congregation. Still not knowing how to handle this situation, I just breathed a quick prayer under my breath, "Lord Help! I don't know what to say!"

Immediately I began to speak; "In case any of you don't know it: That's my youngest daughter."

I paused because that created more laughter. I continued. "Her name is Becca, the oldest one giggling is Elizabeth, and the one with the petrified look on her face is my wife." I paused again. I guess the way I said it created even more laughter.

That was quite an experience that I will always cherish. I was not in no way upset. I was as proud as a daddy could be, because in Becca's childlike innocents, she let everyone know without a shadow of a doubt:

"THAT I WAS HER DADDY!"

JOKES

CAN'T PLEASE THEM ALL

During the preaching a lady kept saying out loud, "um-um-um, you something else." After the service she came out of the door and looked at the preacher and repeated, "um-um-um you something else!" The preacher said, "Mrs. Gladdis, I appreciate the compliment, but you don't have to keep saying that." Well several weeks had passed and Mrs. Gladdis kept saying that. One Sunday after the service was over Mrs. Gladdis came out saying the same thing. The preacher asked, "Mrs. Gladdis, why do you keep saying that?" Mrs. Gladdis replied, "um-um-um you something else cause you certainly ain't no preacher!"

WAIT TILL HE'S SOBER

A man who was trying it get his buddy saved invited him to church. When he went to pick his buddy up, his buddy was drunk. The man decided to take him anyhow hoping something good would come out of it. While they were sitting, listening to the sermon, the preacher said that the "Prayers of a righteous man availeth much". The drunk buddy looked over at his friend and said, "See, I told you it was alright to be drunk." The man replied, "What makes you say that?" The drunk buddy said, "Because of what your preacher just said." The man asked, "What did he say?" The drunk buddy replied, "The preacher said, that the prayers of a fermented man availeth much!"

REDEEMED

While handing a 25-cent-off coupon to the supermarket clerk at the checkout counter, a woman missed her hand and the coupon slipped beneath the scale and was gone. The checker looked distressed, so the woman said, "That's Okay, it's in coupon heaven now." "Coupon heaven?" the checker asked. "Yes", the woman said, "That's where coupons go when they die." "Only the redeemed ones!" said the checker.

HAND SIGNALS

A 3-year-old regularly watched football games with his father so much, that he knew some of the signals the referee makes. On a recent Sunday, the 3-year-old attended church with the family. As the pastor raised his hands high to offer a blessing, the child interrupted the service by shouting, "Touchdown!"

CHILDREN, PLEASE

Yesterday at church, a lady from the congregation was presenting the children's sermon. She walked up to the front of the church and said, "May I have all of the children?" As the children walked forward, several parents responded, "Yes." One quick-witted father asked, "For how long?"

CONSIDER THE SOURCE

When I was a toddler, someone had given me a little tea set as a gift and it was one of my favorite toys. Daddy was in the living room engrossed in the evening news when I brought him a little cup of tea, which was just water. After several cups of tea and lots of praise for such yummy tea, my mom came home. My dad made her wait in the living room to watch his little princess bring him a cup of tea, because it was just the cutest thing! My mom waited, and sure enough, here I come down the hall with a cup of tea for daddy and mom watches him drink it up, and then says, "Did it ever occur to you that the only place that little girl can reach to get water is the toilet?"

IN THE EYES OF A CHILD

A little girl was sitting on her grandfather's lap as he read her a bedtime story. From time to time, she would take her eyes off the book and reach up to touch his wrinkled cheeks. She was alternately stroking her own cheek, then his again. Finally she spoke up, "Grandpa, did God make you?" "Yes, sweetheart," he answered, "God made me a long time ago." "Oh," she paused, "Grandpa, did God make me too?" "Yes, indeed, honey," he said, "God made you just a little while ago." Feeling their respective faces again, she observed, "God's getting better at it, isn't he?"

TYPICAL

A $100 bill and a $1.00 bill met each other and were great friends for quite a long while. One day they were separated and did not see each other for twenty years. When the $1 bill saw the $100 bill, he shouted out, "Hey $100 bill, how are you?" The $100 bill responded with great happiness. The $1 bill asked the $100 bill where he had been all those years. The $100 bill said, "Well I have been to Paris, England, Switzerland, Australia, New York, California," and named many other great places. Then the $100 dollar bill asked, "Well $1 bill, where all have you been?" The $1 bill replied, "Oh just from church to church."

LAST REQUEST

Attending church in Kentucky, we watched an especially verbal and boisterous child being hurried out, slung under his irate father's arm. No one in the congregation so much as raised an eyebrow -- until the child captured everyone's attention by crying out in a charming Southern accent, "Ya'll pray for me now!"

WHO CUT THE CHEESE

A lady had a problem with her husband falling asleep and snoring in church when the preacher started preaching. She went to the pastor to talk to him about it. The preacher said that he did notice that and said that he had an idea on how to keep him from doing that. The preacher told her to get some limburger cheese, take it out of the wrapper and re-wrap it with aluminum foil and put it in her purse. The pastor then told her that when her husband went to sleep and start to snore, to take out the foil, open one end of it and hold it to his nose, "That will wake him up!" Well, the lady did as he said and sure enough, the next service, when the preacher started to preach, her husband went to sleep and started to snore. The lady took out the foil, opened it on one end and held it to his nose. Suddenly the man awoke and without thinking of where he was, he exclaimed, "MYRTLE! GET YOUR FEET OUT FROM UNDER MY NOSE!"

LOSS FOR WORDS

I dreamed that I had gone to Heaven. While standing talking to God, he sneezed. I didn't know what to say.

DADDY'S GONNA EAT YOUR FINGERS

I was packing for my business trip and my three year old daughter was having a wonderful time playing on the bed. At one point she said, "Daddy, look at this" and stuck out two of her fingers. Trying to keep her entertained, I reached out and stuck her tiny fingers in my mouth and said, "Daddy's gonna eat your fingers," pretending to eat them. I went back to packing, looked up again and saw that my daughter was standing on the bed staring at her fingers with a devastated look on her face. I asked, "What's wrong, honey?" She replied, "What happened to my booger?"

Chapter Twelve

WHAT A FART!

In chapter one you read my story about having to open the door for Laurie when we picked her up to go on a youth night at my church. Now, here is the story where I had developed a crush on Laurie and was trying to do everything I could to get Laurie to be my girlfriend.

Laurie was a beautiful girl, with a great smile, charming personality, good looking, slim, long black flowing hair, fun to be with……ok, I hear you, you get the point – I'll move on!

Laurie had a sister named Linda who was about two years younger. The neighborhood kids would usually meet up in their yard to play and have a grand ole time.

I would always try to play where it would allow me to be Laurie's partner in a game so I could hold her hand in a race, or just be close to her in the yard. (I know - I'm getting mushy again).

Unfortunately for me nothing that I did seemed to work. Yes, Laurie liked me but not as her boyfriend. (I wonder if she thought my "quittie shots" were out of date.)

One afternoon I had to stay after school and go into a room to do some make up class work that I had to do. I found that I was not alone; the room was full of other students that needed to do some make up work as well. Now just so you will know, this is taking place when I was in the fifth grade.

I walked into the room and sat down then in came Laurie! My heart was pounding with excitement hoping that she would sit in a seat next to me. Nothing doing. Laurie went to the other side of the classroom and took a seat. My heart returned back to its normal beat and, wow, what a letdown.

I then begin to think that if I could time finishing my work at the same time Laurie had finished hers, I could then walk home with her or if her mother came and picked her up, I could perhaps get a ride home with them - meaning that I would be in the car with Laurie!

The room was so quite as we were doing our work that you could hear a pin drop. I was starting to face a terrible dilemma which turned out to be a very embarrassing situation and very humiliating. But I must confess, looking back on it, it was funny.

There I was sitting in my desk doing my work when I began to feel a sneeze coming on. Well, that's not so bad. This is where the bad comes in; I also felt the compulsion of cumulating gases forming in my stomach looking for a way out as to relieve this unpleasant build up. Folks, simply put: I had to fart. So here I had to sneeze and pass gas at the same time.

Needless to say, I was not successful in sneezing and holding in the other. NO – I sneezed and farted at the same time. At first there was a deadly silence and I thought for a moment that I was going to get by with this. Then, coming from across the room a voice ranged out and said: "Wow, What a Fart!"

Laughter erupted by everyone in there. The teacher in charge of the students got up from her desk and went into the hallway so that I could not see her laugh. I was so embarrassed. And the worst thing about it, Laurie was in the room.

Well, I couldn't concentrate after that and soon I saw Laurie get up, turned in her work and left.

As she was leaving the room there was a slight glance my way and out she went. There went my chance to walk or get a ride home with Laurie.

I never was successful in getting Laurie to be my girlfriend but not too long after that Linda began taking a liking to me and before you knew it, we were boyfriend and girlfriend.

Linda was a beautiful girl, great smile, charming personality, good looking, slim, long blonde flowing hair, fun to be with……ok, I hear you: You get the point!

JOKES

DOUBLE DATE

The head football cheerleader landed a date with the quarter back of the football team. She had been dreaming of the night that he would pick her up and go on a date just the two of them. As the quarterback rung the door bell, she all of a sudden had a strong urge to pass wind (for you rednecks and for those who don't mind – urge to fart).She dared not, so she held it in and opened the door. After the proper greetings to the parents the quarterback escorted her to the car and she got in. As the quarter back was going around she thought; it's now or never. She quickly rolled down the window and passed the gas, it was so forceful that most would call it a caboose explosion! The cheerleader tried her best to fan the ill smelling aroma out of the window with her hands before the quarterback got in. As he opened his door, she quickly rolled the window back up with all hopes that the aroma had left the car. As the quarterback got in he looked at her and said: "By the way, I would like for you to meet the couple in the back seat whom we will be double dating with tonight!"

YOUR FARTS WILL TELL ON YOU

I was in a coffee shop recently when I suddenly realized I desperately needed to fart. The music was really loud so I timed my fart with the beat of the music. After a couple of songs I started to feel better. I finished my coffee and noticed that everyone was looking at me. Suddenly, I remembered that I was listening to my MP3 player.

WHAT'S THE DIFFERENCE

If being born in the United States makes you an American - If being born in France makes you a Frenchman - If being born in England makes you a British, then, what does standing in the restroom make you? European! (your-a-peeing)

POWER FAILER

A lady was sitting in church listening to the sermon. She took out a piece of paper and wrote a note to her husband and handed it to him. He looked at the note and it read, "I just let a silent one, what should I do?" The man wrote a response and handed back to her. She looked at it and it said, "Buy new batteries for your hearing aids."

OLD FART

A cow, ant and old fart (for you young folks, "Old Fart" is a term used to describe an old person) was discussing who was the greatest. The Cow said that she was the greatest because she could give twenty gallons of milk a day. The ant said, "No, no, no, I am the greatest, because I work day and night, and I can carry fifty times my body weight." ---------YOUR TURN! (For you young folks, I'm calling you an old fart and it's your turn to tell why you are the greatest).

WRONG END

A lady went to the doctor because of a personal problem. The doctor came in the examining room and asked the lady about the nature of her problem. She said, "Doctor, every time I pass gas, it don't smell." The doctor said, "WHAT!" The lady repeated, "When I pass gas, it don't smell." Just then, the lady passed some gas and she said, "See, I told you, my toots don't smell." The doctor told the lady that he would be right back and left the room. A few minutes later he returned with a black bag and a nurse. The lady asked, "Oh, are you going to operate on my back side?" The doctor replied, "NO, I'm going to operate on your nose!"

NOW THAT'S BAD

A lady that I use to work with came out of the restroom one day and I said, "I'm not sure what you did in there, but twelve cock roaches came out wearing gas mask and carrying suit cases!

I'M NOT SO SURE HE'S GONE

A man told his wife that when he passed away, he wanted his coffin to be lined with cheese. Years had passed and the day came that her husband passed away. Per her husband's request, his wife had his coffin lined with imported cheese. To keep the cheese from smelling, the coffin was closed and sealed. After the service, the pallbearers began taking the coffin out of the church and down a long flight of stairs to the awaiting hearse. After going down the first few steps, the seal on the coffin broke and the smell of the cheese came out. The man on the back right not knowing what had happened, dropped his part and the coffin began to bump down the steps. One of the pallbearers asked, "Man, why did you let go?" The man replied, "Listen, if that feller has done what I think he has done, He's able to get up and walk himself!"

THE RIGHT PLACE

A boy went to his mother and told her that he was going to go dig a new hole for the outhouse. His mother told him that he didn't have to dig another hole because there was a new way of doing it. She said, "Son, take these three sticks of dynamite. Take one stick and put it in the top part of the outhouse, put the other two in the hole. Then run your cord out of the outhouse and behind a tree. When you push the plunger on the box dentition box, the stick of dynamite in the top of the outhouse will send the outhouse upwards. The two sticks of dynamite in the hole will clean out the hole and fertilize the yard and garden, then, the outhouse will fall back into place. "The son did as instructed. After going behind a tree to hook up his wires, he didn't see Grandma go in the outhouse. He pushed the plunger and everything happened as mother had said. The boy looked around the tree just as the outhouse was coming back down and saw it land on top of Grandma. The boy went running to the outhouse and opened the door and in a frantic voice asked, "GRANDMA, ARE YOU OK?" Grandma replied, "Yes, but I'm sure glad I didn't fart in the kitchen!"

WANTS TO FART

A man took his dad to the nursing home to get him checked in. He helped his dad in a chair and told him that he was going to look for his doctor and then return. While the father was waiting, he started to lean to the right. An orderly came over, caught him and said, "Here sir, let me help you" and he put a pillow between the dad's right side and the arm of the chair. A few moments after the orderly left, the dad started to lean to the left. A nurse came over, caught him and said, "Here sir, let me help you" and she put a pillow between his left side and the arm of the chair. A few moments after the nurse left, the dad started to lean forward. A doctor came over, caught him and said, "Here sir, let me help you" and he put two pillows on his lap. A few moments after the doctor left, the son returned and asked, "Well dad, what do you think of this place so far?" The dad replied, "They are all very nice but they won't let an old man fart!"

TWO COUSINS

A country cousin went to visit her city cousin. One night they were getting ready for a night on the town. The country cousin was watching the city cousin spray cologne from a fancy bottle with one of them plastic spray bulbs. The city cousin seeing her country cousin in the mirror watching her, she turned around and said, "Channel Number five, $50 an ounce." A few minutes later the country cousin was brushing her hair at the mirror when all of a sudden she farted. She saw her city cousin in the mirror with a disgusted look on her face. The country cousin turned around and said, "Butter Beans, $5.00 a bushel!"

DEFINITION OF A FART

Several burps were talking to one another about going outside. One of the burps said to the others, "Why don't we be little stinkers and go out the back door?"

THIS SIDE STORY WAS ADDED BY REQUEST:

I was taking my basic training at Fort Jackson, South Carolina. One morning after breakfast, our platoon was lined up ready to go to the firing range for the days training. Just before we were to move out, one of my fellow solders asked the Drill Sergeant if he could go to the latrine before we moved out. The Drill Sergeant started to yell at him saying, "You were supposed to use the latrine right after 'chow' and before you lined up! Why didn't you?" The Private replied, "I did Drill Sergeant." The Drill Sergeant then asked, "Then why do you have to go again?" The Private said, "Because my farts wasn't farts." The Drill Sergeant in disbelief on what he just heard asked, "What did you say?" The Private repeated what he had said. The Drill Sergeant then asked, "Then what were they?" The Private replied, "They came out like little balls, they weren't farts." The whole platoon broke out into laughter while the Drill Sergeant told the Private to hurry up! The Private grabbed the seat of his pants and ran to the latrine bow legged style. He looked like Fetus on Gun Smoke running toward a gun fight – Bow Legged. It was so funny that the Drill Sergeant had to go inside and laugh it out. Soon the Private returned and all was well. Unfortunately this put us behind on our schedule so we had to run a little faster to make up for lost time – all because of LITTLE BALLS OF FARTS!

Chapter Thirteen

DON'T LICK YOUR PRIVATE PARTS AND THEN TRY TO LICK MY FACE, THEN WE HAVE A DEAL.
(The story on how I got my dog)

I never owned a dog growing up. I've been around them, but never had one.

As a little boy, my friend John had several dogs and they were cute, but I just didn't like them grabbing our baseballs or the toys that we were playing with, with their mouths. They became slimy and I didn't like that.

As I got older, we moved to a new neighborhood and that is where I met my best friend, Matt.

Matt and I became great friends and I can honestly say that we never had a cross word between us. Matt also had a dog. Matt's dog was named "Boots."

"Boots" was your typical dog in many ways except when he walked or ran down the street. When walking or trotting, he kept his front part straight; his hind legs ran at an angle slightly to his right. Only at a full run did he seam to run straight. He looked like this symbol when walking or trotting;

(nose)
\
 \
(hind legs)

Now "Boots" loved to play ball. He would get the ball with his mouth and then it was your turn to chase him. Well, not me. Once that ball became slimmed the game was over for me. To solve this issue, I began to wear gloves so that I didn't have to worry about the slim from then on.

"Boots" did something that dogs do but to me it was horrifying. He would lick his private areas and then do his best to lick me. I didn't have any desire to let that happen. I would run from him when he did that, and "Boots" thought I was playing and would run after me. Of course being a dog, he would catch me. YUK!

So the years have passed and I had gotten remarried and one day my wife called me with the news that she had an opportunity for a dog – FREE. In this case free did not impress me. In my mind I did not want anything to do with a dog. But, listening to her voice and her excitement I agreed to at least meet the dog. There was one condition: she had to bring the dog to me at the church because I was getting ready for an event and I was unable to get away and meet the dog. She agreed.

While my wife was on the way I paused and had a little prayer. It was something like this: "Lord, I don't want a dog. I will be the one having to take care of it and I don't want to. However, I am willing to put my wants aside and be willing to try this for my wife's sake and not mine because she has always had a dog growing up and she wants another one. So, Lord, whatever I need - be it grace and mercy, or whatever, give it to me for her sake."

BE CAREFUL WHAT YOU PRAY FOR!

My wife arrived with the dog. She got out of the car and brought a dog carrier to me and laid it on a table in which I had cleared off for her. She took the dog out and laid the carrier on the floor. He was a very small thing. The dog was just recently weaned from his mother.

There stood that tiny, little dog. He looked at me with his little begging eyes and started to walk to me from across the length of the table with my wife walking with him so that he would not fall off. He came up to me with his little cut off tail just a wagging.

I asked, "What is he doing?" My wife replied, "He wants to meet you." She showed me how to hold out my hand and let him sniff me and we started to get acquainted. I was very nervous but my wife was patient and answered my many questions which seemed to repeat itself: "What's he doing now?" With laughter she would explain.

While looking at the dog I felt something come over me that it is hard to explain. I began to hold the dog and play with him even though he was licking me; I placed him on the floor and in his clumsy little way would follow me. My wife was beside herself. With excitement in her voice she told me that the little dog really liked me. Well, after some more humorous nervousness out of me, I picked the little clumsy dog up and put him back on the table.

He looked up at me and I looked at him and said:

"Here's the deal – **Don't Lick Your Private Parts and Then Try to Lick My Face, I Will Oblige You the Same Then We Have A Deal! You can stay.**

My wife roared with laughter. That little feller licked my hand as if saying, "DEAL!"

I asked my wife if I could name him or does he already have a name. She said his name was Harley but if I wanted to change it I could. I told her that if there ever was a time in my life that I got a dog I would name him, "Roscoe." She very quickly agreed, so Roscoe it was.

Many exciting stories can be shared about my first dog. Roscoe really took up with me and me with him. I took classes on how to work with him and care for him. We really bonded together doing that.

I am single again but I still have Roscoe. He has really been a great medicine to me and the good Lord has used him to help me remember that no matter what happens in life, He is my source and the Lord will provide in all situations.

Children have to be reminded time and time again of things that they are told. Dogs are no different.

Every once in a while, my now grown Rat Terrier that you now know as Roscoe has to be reminded:

Don't Lick Your Private Parts and Then Try to Lick My Face, I Will Oblige You the Same Because We Have A Deal!

JOKES

DUH

A blonde was going to help her husband out by weed eating the yard. In the process of doing so, she accidently cut of the dog's tail. She ran to her neighbor and told her what happened and then requested that the neighbor would let her husband know that she was taking the dog to Walmart. The neighbor asked, "Shouldn't you be taking the dog to the vet?" The blonde replied, "No!"

The neighbor asked, "Why are you taking the dog to Walmart instead of the vet?" The blonde responded by saying, "Because we all know that Walmart is the biggest RETAILER in the country!"

SEX IS A MAN'S BEST FRIEND

Everyone who has a dog calls him 'Rover' or 'Boy'. I call mine 'Sex'. He's a great pal, but he has caused me a great deal of embarrassment.

When I went to City Hall to renew his dog license, I told the clerk that I would like a license for Sex. He said, "I'd like one too!" Then I said, "But this is a dog". He said he didn't care what she looked like. Then I said, "You don't understand, I've had Sex since I was nine years old". He winked and said, "You must have been quite a kid."

When I decided to get married, I told the minister that I wanted to have Sex at my wedding. He told me that I would have to wait until after the wedding. I said, "But Sex has played a big part in my life and my whole lifestyle revolves around Sex." He said he did not want to hear that about my personal life and would not marry us in a church. I told him everyone at the wedding would enjoy having Sex there. The next day, we were married by a justice of the peace. My family has been barred from church.

My wife and I took the dog along with us on the honeymoon. When I checked us into the motel, I told the clerk that I wanted a room for my wife and a special room for Sex. He said, "You don't need a special room, as long as you pay your bill, we don't care what you do." I said, "Look, you don't seem to understand, Sex keeps me awake at night." The clerk said, "Funny -- I have the same problem."

One day I entered Sex in a contest, but before the competition began the dog ran away. Another contestant asked me why I was just standing there, looking all disappointed. I told him I had planned to have Sex in the contest. "I had hoped to have Sex on TV." He said, "Now that cable is all over the place, it's no big deal anymore."

When my wife and I separated, we went to court to fight for the custody of the dog. I said, "Your Honor, I've had Sex before I was married." The judge said, "This courtroom isn't a confessional, stick to the case, please." Then I told him that after I was married, Sex left me. He said that's not unusual. It happens to a lot of people.

Last night, Sex ran off again. I spent hours looking around town for him. A cop came over and asked, "What are you doing in this alley at 4 o'clock in the morning?" I told him I was looking for Sex. My case comes up Thursday.

Well, now I've been thrown in jail, divorced, and had more trouble with that dog than I ever gambled for. The other day, I went for my first visit with a psychiatrist and she asked me, "What seems to be the trouble?" and I replied, "Well, Sex has died and left my life. Its hard losing a best friend and it is so lonely." The doctor said, "Look, You and I both know that sex isn't a man's best friend, so why don't you get yourself a dog?" AURTHOR UNKNOWN

BEST FRIEND

A dog is truly a man's best friend. If you don't believe it, just try this experiment. Put your dog and your wife in the trunk of the car for an hour. When you open the trunk, who is really happy to see you?

THE BIDDING WAR

One day a man went to an auction. While there, he bided on a parrot. He really wanted this bird, so he got caught up in the bidding. He kept on bidding, but kept getting outbid, so he bid higher and higher and higher. Finally, after he bid way more than he intended, he won the bid - the parrot was his at last! As he was paying for the parrot, he said to the auctioneer, "I sure hope this parrot can talk. I would hate to have paid this much for it, only to find out that he can't talk!" "Don't worry," said the auctioneer, "He can talk. Who do you think kept bidding against you?"

THAT STINKS

I was in my car one day listening to a guy on the radio help callers with their home problems. One woman called up hysterical after finding a skunk in her basement. "Leave a trail of bread crumbs or cat food from your basement to your backyard," suggested the show's host. "That'll get rid of it." An hour later the woman called back, even more upset. "Now I have TWO skunks in my basement!"

TOOTH BRUSHES

A man took a job selling tooth brushes. The first night the boss called him and asked how he did. The man said that he had sold 20 tooth brushes. The boss said, "Twenty, that's terrible, you have to do better than that!" The man replied, "I will, you wait and see." The next night the boss called and asked, "How did you do today?" The man said, "I sold 52." The boss said, "Fifty two, that's terrible!" Then the boss said, "Look, I have people selling those tooth brushes by the hundreds and if you can't do any better than this, I will have to replace you." The man said, "Give me one more chance, I'll do better tomorrow." The boss said, "OK, I'll wait and see." The next night the boss called and asked, "How did you do today?"

The man replied, "I SOLD 10,000!!" The boss exclaimed, "TEN THOUSAND! THAT'S A COMPANY RECORD! How in the world did you sell that many?" The man said, "Well, I went to the airport, set up a table with chips and dip at the gates where people got on and off the airplanes. When they came by my table I asked them if they wanted some free chips and dip. They said yes. So, they got them some. After the first bite they said, OOOOH, this taste like dog pooh! I replied, it is, you want to buy a tooth brush?"

WHAT A DOG

A preacher was telling a man in the church that he wanted a dog. The man said that he had just the right dog for him and invited the preacher to his house to see it. The preacher met the man at his house and they went into the living room. The man then called in the dog. The man said, "Now preacher, watch this." The man said, "Rover, go get my King James Bible." The dog went out of the room and in just a few moments came back in with a Bible in its mouth and laid it on the coffee table. The preacher said, "Well, that's alright, but any dog could be trained to do that." The man replied, "Oh, you ain't seen nothing yet." The man said, "Rover, John 3:16." Rover opened the Bible and turned to John 3:16 and laid his paw on it. The preacher said, "Well, that's impressive!" The man then said, "Preacher, you give him a chapter and verse." The preacher said, "Me!" The man said, "Yep." The preacher then said, "OK, Rover, Nehemiah 1:3." Rover turned right to the passage and put his paw on it. The preacher exclaimed, "That's unbelievable!" The man then said, "Preacher, watch this." "Rover: heel!" Rover went over to the chair that the preacher was in, put one front paw on the arm rest and another paw on the preacher's forehead and began to howl – owowowowowowowowowowowow. (In case you're not sure about this one, Rover – Heal)!

I WONDER

Do people who believe in reincarnation call their dogs by saying, "Here, doggie, doggie," or do they say, "Here, uncle, uncle?"

PREACHERS HORSE

A preacher was preparing to travel his circuit and do his ministerial duties. He went to a stable to purchase a horse. The stable owner told the preacher that he had just the horse for him. The stable owner brought him a horse and told him that the horse was a special horse. The stable owner said, "To get the horse to walk all you had to do is to say, Praise the Lord." "To get the horse to go faster just keep saying Praise the Lord with excitement in your voice. The more excitement in the voice, the *faster the horse will run. In order to get the horse to stop, just say Amen."* The preacher got on the horse and said, "Praise the Lord." The horse started to walk. The preacher then said, "Amen" the horse stopped. The preacher bought the horse and the next day the preacher was ready to hit the trail. The preacher said, "Praise the Lord" and the horse started to walk. As the horse was walking down the trail the more excited the preacher got and started to say over and over, "Praise the Lord!" Praise the Lord!" Praise the Lord!" Soon the horse was in a full run. The preacher excited about what was happening, suddenly realized that the trail was going to take a sharp right and if the horse didn't stop they would go over a cliff. The preacher started to say "Whoa! Whoa!" but the horse didn't stop. In the preachers panic he could not remember what to say to get the horse to stop. In last minute desperation the preacher began to pray out loud, asking the Lord to help him in his dilemma. Just as the horse came to the edge of the cliff, the preacher ended his prayer by saying, "AMEN!" The horse came to a complete halt, inches away from going over the cliff. With his hands raised to the sky, with a loud and excited voice the preacher exclaimed, "PRAISE THE LORD!"

WHO'S TRAINING WHO

Two dogs were talking about their owners. One dog asked the other dog, "How is it coming along with your owner?" The dog replied, "Great! Every time I do a trick I have him giving me a treat!"

WHAT'S YOUR NAME

A dog asked the dog next door what his name was. The dog next door replied, "I'm not sure, but I think it is Down Boy."

COLD WATER

A nephew visited his uncle who lived in the mountains. His uncle had a cabin far away from the big cities and was quite content. After supper on the forth night, the nephew volunteered to wash the dishes, so he was going to get some hot water. The uncle said that he didn't need to because cold water would take care of them. The uncle then took all of the dishes and laid them on the floor. The nephew asked, Why are you doing that, and the uncle replied, cold water would get them." Just then the uncle called out, "Cold Water, Come!" A moment later the uncles' dog came in and began licking all of the dishes. The uncle said, "Lets me and you go play cards, he will be finished soon and then we can put up the dishes."

Chapter Fourteen

PLEASE FLUSH!

In every job that I have had there has been all kinds of experiences that I have encountered and I'm sure those of you who are reading this can think of many experiences that you reflect on that makes you laugh.

My current job is no exception to job related experiences.

I was fortunate enough to get a job working in a Chick-fil-a restaurant. I started in the back preparing the food in various positions. During our grand opening there were several people from other Chick-fil-a restaurants that were on hand to help train and oversee the many things that needed to be done. During this time I had several of the trainers asks me if I have ever done this type of work before because they said that I was a natural at it. I told them that not since high school, in which I worked at a Burger King but that only lasted about a month and then my mother decided to move to Griffin, Ga.

Of course, I have had experiences over the years in which I had learned food preparations, and various skills that are used in a restaurant environment. While working in the back an opportunity came about for me to move to Dining Room Host.

We had a dining room hostess and when the times came that she was out I was asked to fill in for her. I remember the first time I went into the dining room I was determined that I was going to make the best of it, just be myself and do the best job that I knew how to do.

A few months have passed and our dining room hostess decided that it was time for her to move on. After she left I was offered the dining room host position and I eagerly accepted. Even though I did well in the back becoming the dining room host became the spot where I was best suited. I'm sure I don't have to list all the numerous things that a dining room host does, (or maybe I should but for the sake of time I won't) but there is one thing that I got initiated on the very first day of being a dining room host.

The first afternoon that I was in the dining room, a boy about six years old was playing in the playground. – Why do we call it a playground? It's inside. Shouldn't we call it a play room?

Oh well, on with the story:

That little six years old decided that it was a long way to the restroom so – standing right in the middle of the room, he unzipped and began the "Golden Arch." For those who don't know what that means, He peed right in the middle of the floor! Well, I had to shut down the playground to scrub and sanitize the floor and let it dry.

The very next morning, a little girl went down the yellow slide and it became obvious that her paper diaper wasn't fastened on tight enough. From the top to the bottom she left a brown trail and it didn't smell good either.

Well, I had to shut down the playground to scrub, sanitize the slide and let it dry. Cleaning the slide presented a different challenge than cleaning a floor. I started at the bottom and began cleaning upward as far as I possibly could. Several times I would slip and slid back down on my knees to the bottom. Climbing inside the slide and trying to keep my footing while it was wet was quite a challenge.

Then came the next challenge. I had to go up through the platform steps of the playground to get to the top of the slide and then clean from the top to where I had left off cleaning from the bottom. Now get this picture in your head: I am lying sideways, holding on for dear life with my left hand while reaching as far as I could with my right hand, my head pointing down that "railroad track" slide praying with all my might that I wouldn't slip. (By the way – "railroad track" meaning poop).

Fortunately I was able to finish the slide without slipping and then went on with my other duties.

Now if that is not enough, the saga continues.

Right after our lunch rush, a boy climbed up the platform stairs to the slide and then sat down at the top. He unzipped and began to make that slide a water fall. He peed all the way down the slide and then climbed back out. OH MY GOODNESS! Here I go again! I had to clean the slide the very same way that I did earlier that morning when cleaning the poop.

In less than twenty four hours of becoming the dining room host I had to scrub, sanitize and dry various parts of the playground three times. To this day I believe I still hold the record for having to clean the playground of bodily functions in a span of less than twenty four hours.

Well, that done it! I cut me a flap off a cardboard box and with a black marker and bold letters, I made me a sign. I shared it with my co-workers and they loved it. Soon the owner/operator came in and I informed him that once again I had to clean the playground. He laughed and gave me his sympathy.

I then told him that I had made a sign and would like to hang it on the playground door. For the record: I knew I wouldn't be able to but I just did this for the humor of it. I showed him my sign and he laughed and did just as I thought – he said no, but he did think it was funny.

On my sign it read:

WHEN YOU ARE FINISHED PLAYING ON THE PLAYGROUND – PLEASE FLUSH.

JOKES

FACTORY WORKERS

In a small town, there is a rather sizable factory that hires only married men. Concerned about this, a local woman called on the manager and asked him, "Why is it you limit your employees to married men? Is it because you think women are weak, dumb, cantankerous, or what?" "Not at all, ma'am," the manager replied. "It is because our employees are used to obeying orders, are accustomed to being shoved around, know how to keep their mouths shut, and don't pout when I yell at them."

THE RAISE

Our boss told us that she is planning a salary raise. One of the guys asked, "When does it become effective?" The boss answered, "As soon as you do."

COMMUNICATION DEVICES

Three women, two younger, and one senior citizen, were sitting in a sauna. Suddenly there was a beeping sound. One of the younger women pressed her forearm and the beep stopped. The other two looked at her questioningly. "That was my pager," she said. "I have a microchip under the skin of my arm." A few minutes later, a phone rang. The second young woman lifted her palm to her ear. When she finished, she explained, "That was my mobile phone. I have a microchip in my hand." The older woman felt very low tech. Not to be out done, she decided she had to do something just as impressive. She stepped out of the sauna and went to the bathroom. She returned with a piece of toilet paper hanging from the back of her swimsuit. The others raised their eyebrows and stared at her. The older woman finally said........."well, will you look at that...I'm getting a fax!"

DOT WORKER

A man took on a job at the Department of Transportation (DOT) painting lines on county roads. The man was given a *paint bucket, a brush and shown where to start. On Monday the man painted 1 mile stretch of road. On Tuesday the man painted ¾ mile stretch of road. On Wednesday the man painted ½ mile of road. On Thursday the man only painted 500 feet. When the worker returned Friday morning his supervisor shared about his concern on how little of road is getting painted later in the week and was wondering what the problem was. The man quickly replied, "I'm getting further away from my paint can!"*

RECOGNITION

Peeing in your black or navy blue pants is like doing a good job at work; you get a warm feeling, but no one ever notices.

NEVER TOO OLD TO LEARN

There are three very important things I have learned working in a dining room. 1) Never ask a lady how old she is, 2) never ask a lady when she is due, 3) never ask a lady if her drink is diet.

BIRTHDAY CELEBRATION

Four Ladies celebrating their 50th birthday together went to their favorite restaurant because the waiters where really "HOT." When they turned 60, they went to their favorite restaurant because the food was really good. When they turned 70, they went to their favorite restaurant because it had great handicap parking. When they turned 80, they went to their favorite restaurant for the first time.

NEW WASHING MACHINE

A mother wrote her son who was in the military about the new house they had bought. Part of her letter that she wrote said, "And son, this house came with a new washing machine. The only thing I don't like about it is that every time you push the handle down the cloths disappear.

WASH YOUR HANDS

A Marine was in the latrine using the urinal when an Army soldier came in and began using the other urinal. When the Marine got finished, he went to the sink and began to wash his hands. Soon the Army soldier was finished and headed for the door. The Marine said, "Hey Army man, didn't your drill sergeant teach you to wash your hands after using the latrine?" The Army soldier replied, "Nope, he taught us not to get it on our hands."

WORTH THE EFFORT

A Marine and Army soldier were using a two seater porta johnny while on joint field maneuvers. When the Army soldier was finished, he dropped a quarter down in the hole. The Army soldier then took out his wallet and took out a $100 bill and threw it in the hole. The Marine with a shocked looked and questionable voice asked, "Why on earth did you throw that $100 bill in that hole?" The Army soldier replied, "You don't expect me to go down there just for a quarter do you?"

HONEST ABE

Abraham Lincoln was known as honest Abe. The way he got that name was, one day his father came to him and asked,

"Abe, did you push the outhouse over the hill and down into the creek today?" Abe replied, "Yes father, I did." Abe's father said, "Then you and I are going to the wood shed." Abe said, "But father, George Washington told the truth about chopping down the cherry tree and didn't get a whooping, why am I getting a whopping?" Abe's father replied, "Because George Washington's father wasn't in that tree!"

DON'T FLUSH

A man who was checking in a motel in Texas couldn't wait to get to his room to use the restroom, so he asked the attendant for the directions to the nearest restroom. The attendant told him to go down the hall and turn left and the first door on the right will be the restroom. The man started to walk down the hall and noticed how long it was. He also noticed how big everything in Texas was while coming from the airport to the motel. He had heard that everything in Texas was bigger than anywhere else he would travel to. The hallway was so long, he forgot the directions he was given. Instead of turning left, he went to his right and walked in the first door on the left and straight into the indoor pool. He began to shout, "Don't Flush! Don't Flush!"

Chapter Fifteen

TINA – YOU MIGHT WANT TO EXPLAIN THAT!

A church that I once attended decided to do a major Easter production showing the best that could be shown on a stage of what it was going to be like living on earth after the rapture of the church and the story of the death and resurrection of Christ all in the same drama.

I was asked to be the prop team coordinator and also to play a role in the drama as the false prophet that is mentioned in the book of Revelations in the Bible.

As the false prophet I was to call fire down from the heavens, which included filming a segment to be played during the drama and to also perform live on stage.

Performing live on stage and being the prop team coordinator presented a unique challenge.

To make this challenge better understood let me tell you about being the prop team coordinator.

By working closely with the drama coordinator (that's what we called the person in charge) I had to find or create all of the props used in the drama. I had to also know all the ends and outs of all the staging, where all of the actors where suppose to be, and so on.

Tony was in charge of the constructing the stages. He also built several of the prop items that were used. Needless to say we worked closely together to make sure everything coordinated as it was suppose to.

Tina (Tony's wife) had an acting part in the drama and was the prop room coordinator. She made sure that all of the props where in their assigned spot and readied the props as they were called for during the drama.

Being on the prop team we had to dress in total black so that when we were on stage we were hard to see. I wore a black hat, black shirt, t-shirt, pants, socks, boots, gloves, hunters vest, with a military style black belt and buckle. I also wore dark underwear just in case my pant fell down. JUST KIDDING!

Now with all of this said, here was the challenge.

As prop coordinator I had to wear all black. On stage as one of the actors, I had to wear a suit. That meant that before my time on stage I was in all black, while on stage I was in a suit and after my part on stage I had to get back into my all black again. I had about thirty seconds after coming off the stage to go from a suit to all black because I had to run and place props on a section of the stage which was on the other side.

Superman I am not. Even if I were superman we didn't have anywhere to put a phone booth for me to run in and change like superman.

I then came to the realization that I had to practice changing in order to be ready in about thirty seconds after coming off the stage. The first practice run took me two and half minutes. That wasn't going to work. After a few adjustments it took about two minutes. That wasn't going to work. After some more adjustments I got it down to one and half minutes. That still wasn't good enough.

Well, my good friend Todd, who was also part of the prop team offered to help and we came up with an idea.

I decided that I would put my suit on over my prop outfit. With a coat on no one would even notice that my dress pants weren't buttoned and that the zipper was down. The belt kept them up and closed enough to wear. I found a white shirt larger from the size that I wore and put it on over my black shirt. (I had to leave the vest off). I already had black socks so that wasn't a problem. My dress shoes that I wore were loosely tied. They were tied just enough to keep them on but loose enough that I could kick them off without un-tying them. I kept my hair short so that I could comb my hair quickly to go on stage and it looked right. One more thing, I had to wear a miniature lapel mic while on stage and once off stage return to my two head sets that I wore. One head set was to keep in contact with the director and the other one was to keep in contact with the prop team. So, the sound team put the lapel mic on me in such a way that when I came off stage I could get it off with just a few seconds.

Now the time had come to practice doing all of this before we actually got started practicing the drama.

Tina had a stop watch to time me and Todd. On your mark, get set, GO! I exited the stage, went down three steps and by that time I had the lapel mic off and shoved it in the sound team member's hand. I ran to the prop room and quickly got out of my on stage clothing, put on my boots and tied them, put on my vest, put on both head sets and then my hat. One minute. After a few adjustments we had the second run. Forty-Five seconds, after several more adjustments and practice I finally got it down to twenty to twenty five seconds!!

Tina was laughing for all that it was worth. She was so excited that I had mastered changing that fast. Tina then said, "I'm going to bring a tape for my video camera tomorrow night and film you changing."

The next night, Tony, Tina, and I were in the prop room getting ready for the evening practice.

Tony had to leave and go take care of some things, I was in one of the corners of the prop room getting some props ready and Tina was in the opposite corner setting up her camera.

One of the ladies in the drama, Pam came by to say hi. She poked her head in the door and greeted me and then looked over and greeted Tina. Pam seeing that the video camera was pointing toward me made her curious. Pam asked, "Tina, what's the camera pointing toward Gerald for?" Tina in her own innocent way, with that sweet mellow high pitch voice looked at Pam and said, "I'm going to film Gerald stripping."

I looked straight at Pam to see her reaction because I knew what Tina was meaning but Pam sure didn't! Pam's lower jaw had dropped all the way to the floor and her face showed total shock! Pam could not say a word! I looked over at Tina to see if she had figured out how that sounded but it didn't dawn on her what-so-ever the impact of that statement.

I looked back at Pam who still was in total shock, looked back down at the prop I was preparing and with the calmest voice I knew how I replied, "Tina, you might want to explain that." All along I was trying my best not to burst out laughing. I didn't want Tina to be embarrassed.

Tina asked, "Explain what?" She looked at Pam and saw the shock on her face and then it dawned on her what she had just said and how it sounded and that Pam had no idea what-so-ever what was going on.

Tina replied, "OH NO, let me explain!" After explaining what was going on Pam's face recovered from the shock and we all had a good laugh. At that time Tony returned and seeing us laughing asked what was so funny.

Pam looked at Tony and said, "You don't need to leave this prop room anymore, otherwise your wife is going to film Gerald stripping!" Pam walked off. By now, Tony had a be- withered look on his face as he looked at me, which by now I had the look of shock on my face but at the same time laughing, Tony looked at Tina who was busting a gut laughing so hard, Tina then looked at me and then I said to her,"

"TINA, YOU MIGHT WANT TO EXPLAIN THAT!"

JOKES

THE BLONDE AND THE VOICE

A blonde wanted to go ice fishing. She'd seen many books on the subject, and finally getting all the necessary tools together, she made for the ice. After positioning her comfy stool, she started to make a circular cut in the ice. Suddenly, from the sky, a voice boomed, "THERE ARE NO FISH UNDER THE ICE." Startled, the blonde moved further down the ice, and began to cut yet another hole. Again from the heavens the voice bellowed, "THERE ARE NO FISH UNDER THE ICE." The blonde, now worried, moved away, clear down to the opposite end of the ice. She set up her stool once more and tried again to cut a hole. The voice came once more, "THERE ARE NO FISH UNDER THE ICE." She stopped, looked skyward, and said, "Is that you, Lord? " The voice replied, "NO, THIS IS THE MANAGER OF THE HOCKEY RINK."

ALL IN THE TIMING

There was a preacher who always wanted the songs sung in church to go along with the flow of the service and on what he was going to preach on. One Sunday morning he noticed that a Sister Gloria, who was always on time, never late, who always sat in the second pew to the pulpits right, wasn't there. He knew that he could not hold up the service waiting on her, so he began. The preacher had everyone turn in their hymnbooks to page 87 and all sing, "Leaning on the Everlasting Arms," when in walked Sister Gloria carrying her usual stack of books which consisted of her Bible Concordance, Topical Bible, Bible Dictionary, note book for taking sermon notes, and on top was her Bible. The preacher also realized why she was late. It was obvious that she had been in the restroom, because on top of all of that was a roll of toilet paper. In her rush, Sister Gloria, unconsciously put it on top and went straight to the sanctuary. Sister Gloria made her way all the way to the second pew and noticed that someone was sitting in her seat. As she leaned over to ask them to move over the roll of toilet paper fell off her Bible, hit the floor, and began to un-ravel as it rolled toward the front. The toilet paper came to an abrupt halt right in front of the pulpit. Of course everyone in the church, including the preacher saw what was going on, so once Sister Gloria was seated, the preacher said, "Instead of singing on page 87, let's turn to page 197 and sing, "When the Roll Is Called Up Yonder."

COOKING INSTRUCTIONS

Every Sunday the choir would sing their special song just before the preacher would preach the sermon. Every time the choir would start singing, the choir director noticed that two ladies, who sat up front, would start talking to each other. The choir director shared his concerns with the pastor, who in turn talked to the two ladies asking them not to talk during the choir's special. Unfortunately, it didn't do any good. The very next time the choir started to sing, the two ladies would start talking to each other. During the next choir practice, the choir director worked with the choir so much that at any given time when he gave the sign to stop signing, they immediately stopped, and the music stopped playing. Sure enough, the next Sunday came and as the choir began to sing, the two ladies once again started to talk to each other. The song that the choir was singing was very jubilant and right at the point that the song was fast paced and high notes where being sung and played, the two ladies had to talk louder so that they could hear each other. Right at that moment the choir director gave the sign and the singing and music came to a sudden stop. The lady doing the talking didn't notice that all had come to a complete silence, and she was heard by all as she said, "**I COOK MY CHICKEN IN CRISCO, WHAT DO YOU COOK YOURS IN?**"

RECEPTIONIST

A lady with an unusual name was hired to answer the phone in a certain department of the hospital. Within a couple of calls, it was obvious that it was not going to work out. The ladies name was Peek-A-Boo. She was assigned to the ICU unit. When she answered the phone she would say, "Peek-A-Boo, ICU"

ALMOST GOT ME

A pilot of a bi-plane went to the country in order to introduce flying to the farmers and their families. Upon landing in a field, many people from all over came out to see the airplane. After talking to the people, he offered rides for $25 each. Many of the people took the pilot up on his offer. When everyone had gotten their ride, the pilot noticed an older couple who have been there all day long but never made any effort to ride the plane. The pilot went over to them and asked if they were interested in a ride. The man said, "No, not at $50.00." After explaining why that was a fair price, the man still said no. Finally the pilot said, "I'll tell you what, if you and your wife take a ride with me and neither one of you yell out in fear, I won't charge you the fee, however, if either one of you yell out, then you have to pay me the $50.00." The man and his wife agreed and so they boarded the plane. The pilot did every move with the plane that he possibly could, including flying upside down. No matter what he did, the pilot could not get the couple to yell out. Finally the pilot landed and told the man that he thought for sure that he could get them to yell but he couldn't, so therefore he did not have to pay. The man replied, "Well sonny, don't be too hard on yourself, because, you almost got me on that last fly by upside down when my wife fell out."

JUST DON'T GET IT

A couple having a glitch in life decided to get help from a counselor to see if he could help. After five minutes of talking, the counselor said, "I see exactly what the problem is." He got up from his chair and went around to where the woman was sitting. He had her to stand and then gave her the biggest kiss ever imagined. The counselor then helped her back in her chair, went back to his chair and sat down. The he leaned toward the man and said, "Now, that is what your wife needs at least three times a week. The counselor asked, "Sir, do you understand what I am saying?" The man said, "Yes, now I play golf on Tuesdays and Thursdays, so I will bring her in, Mondays, Wednesdays and Fridays.

A NEW DAY DAWNING

A man in an office was dating a girl that he really admired whose name was Loraine.

One day while sitting in his office, a new girl was brought in to be introduced to him; her name was Clearly. The moment that the man saw Clearly, he completely fell in love with her and began to come up with ways to start dating her. His only problem was how he could stop dating Loraine without hurting her. One day, Loraine came to him and said that she was going to be leaving the country for about two years and asked that they put a hold their dating. When Loraine left, the man was so excited, that as he was walking back to his office he begin to sing, "I can see Clearly now Loraine is gone, it's going to be a bright – bright sun shinny day, it's going to be a bright – bright sun shinny day!

CHECK AND DOUBLE CHECK - WHEN A WEDDING IS CONCERN TRIPLE CHECK

A couple was arranging their wedding and told the bakery that they wanted the scripture "1 John 4:18" inscribed on their cake. The verse reads, "There is no fear in love. But perfect love drives out fear..." The bakery somehow got it wrong and put John 4:18 on the cake. The verse reads, "The fact is, you have had five husbands, and the man you now have is not your husband."

KEEP UP WITH YOUR CELL PHONE

Several men were in a locker room after a round of golf. One of the golfers went to the showers and left his cell phone on the bench. The phone rang and another golfer answered it and put it on speaker phone. This is how the phone call went.

MAN: "Hello"

WOMAN: "Honey, I'm at the mall and found a beautiful leather coat that cost $1000.00, can I buy it?"

MAN: "Sure, if it will make you happy, buy the coat."

WOMAN: "Oh thank you honey! By the way, I also saw that the car at the Mercedes dealership that I wanted has been discounted to $75,000.00, Can I go ahead and buy it too?"

MAN: "By all means, and make sure that it has all of the options included."

WOMAN: "Honey, you're the greatest!" "Dear, one more thing, the house that we were looking at, well, they are only asking $420,000.00 for it, what do you think?"

MAN: "Well, then go ahead and put an offer on it."

WOMAN: "OK, honey, you're the greatest, I will see you later!"

The man hung up the phone. Then he looked at the other men who were looking him in complete shock. Then the man asked, "Whose phone is this?"

PROMOTION

For the last five years I have been the back end of the donkey, in the donkey suit, for our Christmas play at church. I was listening to a preacher who was saying that this was the year for *my promotion; God was going to promote me for my diligence in serving him. I raised my hands to the sky and said, "Lord, I receive, Lord I believe this is the year for my promotion!" Two days later I got a call from our Christmas play director, saying, that this year I am going to be promoted in the Christmas play! This year I am going to be the front of the donkey! Praise the Lord; I am going to be the head and not the tail!"*

DON'T DO MY PART

Last year during the Christmas play rehearsal, I was the back end of the donkey and in doing that, I had to bend over and hold the waist of the one doing the front of the donkey. Shortly after coming on stage I had to come out of that suit. Thank God that is was fasten together with Velcro. I came out of that suit, hit that guy upside his donkey head and said, "Whew! Brother, that's my part!" (He passed gas).

GARTER SNAKES CAN BE DANGEROUS

Snakes known as Garter Snakes (Thamnophissirtalis) can be dangerous. Yes, grass snakes, not rattlesnakes. Here's why.
A couple in Sweetwater, Texas, had a lot of potted plants. During a recent cold spell, the wife was bringing a lot of them indoors to protect them from a possible freeze. It turned out that a little green garden grass snake was hidden in one of the plants. When it had warmed up, it slithered out and the wife saw it go under the sofa. She let out a very loud scream.
The husband (who was taking a shower) ran out into the living room naked to see what the problem was. She told him there was a snake under the sofa. He got down on the floor on his hands and knees to look for it. About that time the family dog came and cold-nosed him on the behind. He thought the

snake had bitten him, so he screamed and fell over on the floor. His wife thought he had had a heart attack, so she covered him up, told him to lie still and called an ambulance.

The attendants rushed in, would not listen to his protests, loaded him on the stretcher, and started carrying him out. About that time, the snake came out from under the sofa and the Emergency Medical Technician saw it and dropped his end of the stretcher. That's when the man broke his leg and why he is still in the hospital.

The wife still had the problem of the snake in the house, so she called on a neighbor who volunteered to capture the snake. He armed himself with a rolled-up newspaper and began poking under the couch. Soon he decided it was gone and told the woman, who sat down on the sofa in relief. But while relaxing, her hand dangled in between the cushions, where she felt the snake wriggling around. She screamed and fainted, the snake rushed back under the sofa.

The neighbor man, seeing her lying there passed out, tried to use CPR to revive her. The neighbor's wife, who had just returned from shopping at the grocery store, saw her husband's mouth on the woman's mouth and slammed her husband in the back of the head with a bag of canned goods, knocking him out and cutting his scalp to a point where it needed stitches.

The noise woke the woman from her dead faint and she saw her neighbor lying on the floor with his wife bending over him, so she assumed that the snake had bitten him. She went to the kitchen and got a small bottle of whiskey, and began pouring it down the man's throat. By now, the police had arrived.

(BREATHE HERE)!

They saw the unconscious man, smelled the whiskey, and assumed that a drunken fight had occurred. They were about to arrest them all, when the women tried to explain how it all *happened over a little garden snake! The police called an ambulance, which took away the neighbor and his sobbing wife.*

Now, the little snake again crawled out from under the sofa and one of the policemen drew his gun and fired at it. He missed the snake and hit the leg of the end table. The table fell over, the lamp on it shattered and, as the bulb broke, it started a fire in the drapes. The other policeman tried to beat out the flames, and fell through the window into the yard on top of the family dog who, startled, jumped out and raced into the street, where an oncoming car swerved to avoid it and smashed into the parked police car.

Meanwhile, neighbors saw the burning drapes and called in the fire department. The firemen had started raising the fire ladder when they were halfway down the street. The rising ladder tore out the overhead wires, put out the power, and disconnected the telephones in a ten-square city block area (but they did get the house fire out).

Time passed! Both men were discharged from the hospital, the house was repaired, the dog came home, the police acquired a new car and all was right with their world.

A while later they were watching TV and the weatherman announced a cold snap for that night. The wife asked her husband if he thought they should bring in their plants for the night.

The husband not saying a word, got his shot gun, went outside and shot all of the potted plants. Seeing that there weren't any snakes he looked at is wife and said, "Now you can!"

Chapter Sixteen

YOU MIGHT JUST HAVE THE CALLING YOU MIGHT NOT BE READY FOR YOUR CALLING

Several years ago at a former church I was ask to do a comic routine for our Christmas dinner.

I got my inspiration on what I did that night from Jeff Foxworthy doing his, "You Know you're a Redneck If:"

I did a comic routine followed by a list of thing describing if you might just have the "Calling" or you might not be ready for your "Calling."

Now for you folks that don't know what it means to have the "Calling," let me explain for you. Asking someone if they have the "Calling" simply means, do they feel a tug in their hearts from God to become a minister of the Gospel – to become a preacher. So from that, folks just simply asked: "Brother, do you have the calling?" This is understood dialogue with a lot of southern people.

So at the Christmas dinner I addressed the issue, how do you know if you have the calling and are you ready for it.

So, grab a pew, and find out if you have the calling or not!

YOU MIGHT JUST HAVE THE CALLING
(YMJHTC)

IF

WHEN YOU PREACH IN THE SHOWER AND THE HOT AND COLD KNOBS, AND SHOWER HEAD GET SAVED, *YMJHTC*

WHEN AT THE SUPPER TABLE YOU ARE HANDED A PLATE AND YOU PUT MONEY ON IT, *YMJHTC*

WHEN YOU GET YOUR MOTHERS BLESSINGS AND YOUR DAD HANDS YOU THE CAR KEYS WITHOUT OBJECTION, *YMJHTC*

WHEN YOU GO TO THE ALTAR EVERY SERVICE AND PEOPLE BEGAN CALLING YOU THE ALTAR BOY, *YMJHTC*

WHEN YOU'RE AT THE SUPPER TABLE AND YOU'RE ASKED TO GIVE THE BLESSING AND YOU PRAY OUTLOUD, CHICKEN! ARISE, *YMJHTC*

YOU DUNK YOURSELF IN THE TUB BEFORE YOU GET OUT THINKING YOU ARE BAPTISING YOURSELF, *YMJHTC*

IF YOU HAVE A CHICKEN INSTEAD OF A DOG FOR A PET, *YMJHTC*

IF YOU CAN'T WAIT FOR THE NEXT CHURCH DINNER SO YOU CAN HAVE SOMETHING FLOATING IN GREASE, BECAUSE YOU THINK GREASE IS YOUR BEST FRIEND, *YMJHTC*

IF YOU CAN SPELL JOSHAPHAT AND DEUTERONOMY WITHOUT LOOKING IT UP, *YMJHTC*

IF YOU CAN PRONOUNCE EVERY NAME AND PLACE IN THE BIBLE WITHOUT FLAW, *YMJHTC*

THE FIRST THING YOU REACH FOR IN A MOTEL ROOM IS THE GIDEON BIBLE INSTEAD OF THE REMOTE CONTROL, *YMJHTC*

WHEN RIDING DOWN A ROAD AND YOU SEE A SIGN THAT SAYS "BLIND DRIVEWAY AHEAD" AND YOU STOP, GET OUT AND PRAY THE PRAYER OF HEALING OVER IT, *YMJHTC*

IF YOU ORDER A PRAISE AND WORSHIP MEAL INSTEAD OF A HAPPY MEAL AT MCDONALD, *YMJHTC*

IF YOUR PENTECOSTAL AND YOUR UPSET THAT THERE ISN'T A CHANDELIER HANGING IN THE SANCTUARY FOR YOU TO SWING ON WHEN YOU GET EXCITED, *YMJHTC*

IF YOU CAN GARGLE JUST AS I AM WITH MOUTHWASH, *YMJHTC*

IF YOU SIT AND WATCH THE 12:00 ON YOUR VCR BLINK AND BLINK THINKING THAT THE VERY NEXT BLINK COULD MEAN THAT THE RAPTURE MAY TAKE PLACE, *YMJHTC*

YOU MIGHT NOT BE READY FOR YOUR CALLING (YMNBRFYC)

IF

WHEN THE PASTOR IS PREACHING ON THE HOLY GHOST AND FIRE AND YOU DIAL 911 TO SUMMON THE FIREMEN, *YMNBRFYC*

WHEN YOU FIND OUT THAT YOUR MOTHER-IN-LAW IS COMING TO STAY FOR A MONTH AND YOU START REBUKING SATAN, *YMNBRFYC*

AFTER YOUR MOTHER- IN- LAW PACKS UP, GETS IN HER CAR AND GOES DOWN THE ROAD OUT OF SIGHT AND YOU NO LONGER HEAR HER CAR AND YOU START SINGING, WE HAVE HEARD THE JOYFUL SOUND JESUS SAVES, JESUS SAVES, MY MOTHER- IN -LAW SHE JUST LEFT TOWN, JESUS SAVES, JESUS SAVES! *YMNBRFYC*

IF YOU'RE ASKED TO TURN TO A BOOK IN THE BIBLE AND YOU HAVE TO GO TO THE TABLE OF CONTENTS TO SEE WHAT PAGE IT IS ON, *YMNBRFYC*

IF YOU THINK THE BOOK OF JOB IS THE BOOK OF "JOB" (as in work), *YMNBRFYC*

IF YOU THINK THE CONCORDANCE IS ONE OF THE BOOKS IN THE BIBLE, *YMNBRFYC*

IF YOU PLAN TO PREACH YOUR FIRST SERMON OUT OF THE BOOK OF CONCORDANCE, *YMNBRFYC*

IF YOU THINK THAT BURGER KING IS A PART TIME BUSINESS FOR JESUS, *YMNBRFYC*

IF YOU THINK THAT GOLDEN CORRAL IS WHERE JESUS IS KEEPING THE HORSE THAT HE IS GOING TO RETURN ON WHEN HE COMES BACK TO KICK SATANS REAR ONCE AND FOR ALL, *YMNBRFYC*

IF YOU THINK THAT A MIGHTY RUSHING WIND IS SOMETHING YOU DO AFTER EATING A BURITTO AND A BOWL FULL OF HOT CHILI AND BEANS, *YMNBRFYC*

IF YOU THINK THE TABLETS THAT GOD GAVE MOSES WERE ALKERSELTZERS, *YMNBRFYC*

IF YOU THINK ROLLER COASTERS ARE ALTERNATE MEANS OF SCARING THE DEVIL OUT OF SOMEONE TO GET THEM SAVED, *YMNBRFYC*

IF YOU THINK THE BOOK OF HEBREWS IS INSTRUCTIONS FOR MEN TO MAKE COFFEE AT HOME, *YMNBRFYC*

IF YOU THINK THE LAYING ON OF HANDS IS ANOINTING YOUR KNUCKLES WITH OIL AND SQUARING YOUR NEIGHBOR RIGHT IN THE NOSE AFTER HE HAS UPSET YOUR DAY, *YMNBRFYC*

IF YOU THINK JOHN 3:16 IS THE MEN'S ROOM ON THE THIRD FLOOR, *YMNBRFYC*

IF YOU THINK BED, BATH AND BEYOND IS SYMBOLIC OF HEAVEN, *YMNBRFYC*

IF YOU THINK THAT GALATIANS 5:22, 23 IS TALKING ABOUT FRUIT OF THE LOOMS, *YMNBRFYC*

AND, "IF AFTER YOU HAVE HAD DEVOTIONS WITH YOUR FAMILY, THEY BOW THEIR HEADS , AND RIGHT BEFORE YOU PRAY, YOU LOOK OVER THINKING YOUR LOOKING AT YOUR PIANIST AND ORGANIST AT YOUR CHURCH AND SAY,

"COME PLAY SOFTLY",

YOU MIGHT JUST HAVE THE CALLING!!!!!!!!!!

IF YOU THINK THAT ALL OF THIS IS ACTUAL WAYS OF KNOWING IF YOU ARE READY FOR YOU CALLING OR NOT,

YOU AIN'T READY FOR YOUR CALLING!

Chapter Seventeen

I DON'T CARE WHAT YOU PLAY, YOU GET THEM IN AND YOU GET THEM OUT! THAT'S AN ORDER!!

I'm quite amazed on how I can try my best to stay out of trouble and avoid situations that I don't want to be in, but yet, I find myself getting in trouble and getting into situations that I don't want to be in. Can someone please tell me how that works!

This story is about a situation I found myself in, wondering how did I get there in the first place.

It takes place when I was a Chapel Activities Specialist, at Headquarters and Headquarters Company, 426th Signal Battalion, 35th Signal Group, Fort Bragg, North Carolina.

I was assigned to assist our Group Chaplain, Chaplain Smith, at a wedding to be held in our Group Chapel. It was my duties of a Chaplain Assistant to arrive early and prepare the Chapel for the wedding ceremony.

The wedding was going to be very small as far as attendance was concerned. So, this was to be a very short, sweet and simple ceremony.

In every wedding, no matter how big or small the thought of something going wrong is on the minds of most everyone. You would think that a wedding consisting of no more than fifteen people –including the Bride and Groom – nothing could go wrong. WRONG!

Thirty minutes before the wedding, Chaplain Smith came into the office I was in with a very worried look on his face. I could tell how he was acting that something was troubling him. I asked, "Sir, what's wrong?" Chaplain Smith told me that the organist hasn't arrived and he was getting worried. I tried to console him by reminding him that our organist was very faithful and on time and not to worry. I was certain that she had a slight delay.

Chaplain Smith looked at me and thanked me, and went out. About fifteen minutes before the wedding I was beginning to be concerned. It was not like the organist to be this late. I had already begun to think on what to do if she didn't show up. About this time Chaplain Smith found me again and I informed him that I tried to call her house but there was no answer. I suggested that we give it another five minutes. After the five minutes was up, Chaplain Smith asked me if I had any suggestions. I told him that I have been trying to think of anyone else that played the organ, but I did not know of anyone. I was a complete loss at what to do.

Chaplain Smith paused and then looked me straight in the eye and asked, "Cooper, do you play the organ?" I replied no Sir; I don't play the organ I just goof around with them." Honey, I should have left that last part out!

Chaplain Smith asked me what I meant by goofing around with them. I said, "Well Sir; I have come up here to the Chapel in the evenings and played the organ with one finger while using the buttons on it to make sounds that went along with what I was playing.

He quickly replied: "Cooper you're my organist!" I said, "No Sir, I can't do that! I have never played in front of anyone and I didn't want to mess things up!" Chaplain Smith then asked if I have ever played the Wedding March. I replied yes but with only one finger and I'm not sure if I could remember how to play it all.

Chaplain Smith then said: "Cooper, you're my organist! I don't care what you play; you just get them in there and get them out!" I said, "But Sir!".... Chaplain Smith interrupted and said, "THAT'S AN ORDER!"

Folks when a Chaplain who is also an Army Major says "That's an Order" all discussion is over and I became an Official, Un-Learned, Un-Rehearsed, Very Nervous - Army - Military Wedding Organist!

I went up front and took my place on the bench. My hands where so sweaty by the time I got to the organ, that I had to rub them on my pants several times to dry them.

I turned the organ on, set a few of the buttons for some special effects, pressed a few notes to find the beginning of the Wedding March and there I was, ready as I was ever going to be.

You should have seen the shock look on my Company Commanders and First Sergeants faces when I sat down at the organ. I looked at them, gave them a look of "SAVE ME, GET ME OUT OF HERE" which was to no avail. They couldn't believe that it was me at the organ.

Well, Chaplain Smith came down front and took his place. I was praying in my mind all this time, "LORD, TELL GOD THAT THIS WOULD BE A GREAT TIME FOR THE RAPTURE TO TAKE PLACE! IF NOT THE RAPTURE, LET'S JUST PRACTICE AND TAKE ME UP AND DROP ME OFF ON THE ROOF, I WILL TAKE IT FROM THERE!"

Well, needless to say that didn't happen. Just then, Chaplain Smith looked at me and nodded. With a great big breath I started to play the Wedding March. Fortunately for me the chapel wasn't very big and I only had to play the first verse. I didn't have to play it twice. When the Bride and Groom had reached the front I was finished! And believe it or not, I was in rhythm with their pace and I did quite well without any mistakes – USING ONLY ONE FINGER - with sound effects buttons!

Chaplain Smith looked at me with the biggest smile on his face. I glanced at the Company Commander and First Sergeant and they had a look of surprise on their faces. They couldn't believe that I actually did that. Quite frankly, neither could I believe it!

Well, after a sigh of relief, I sat there and all of a sudden I had a "Brain Freeze." I could not for the life of me remember the tune to play for the Bride and Groom to walk back down the aisle once they were pronounced husband and wife, "You may now kiss your Bride."

Very quietly, I started to hum hoping that something would stir my memory and I would remember the tune, but nothing I did was helping. The part for pronouncing them Husband and Wife was fast approaching and I still could not think of that tune.

I then decided that I wouldn't play anything. I would just sit there and smile as the newlywed couple was leaving. But, then more horror set in when I remembered the last words of the Chaplain before going in. "I DON'T CARE WHAT YOU PLAY; YOU JUST GET THEM IN THERE AND GET THEM OUT, THAT'S AN ORDER!"

The part then came when Chaplain Smith pronounced the couple Husband and Wife and told the Groom he may kiss his Bride. He had them turn and introduced them by their new title; Mr. and Mrs.

Chaplain Smith then looked at me and nodded. I was horrified, I tried to tell him I didn't know what to play but he gave me the look that if I don't play something I was going to die!

And then it happened. A tune came in my mind and I began to play. On the way out the Bride and Groom looked back at me with a look of horror and bewilderment. Chaplain Smith, the Company Commander, First Sergeant, and the few present was looking at me with the same looks.

I knew without a doubt that when this was over I was going to be sent straight to Fort Leavenworth. I was so nervous that sweat was pouring down my back.

After the Bride and Groom had exited, I stopped playing and bowed my head. Chaplain Smith came over to me and asked, "Cooper, what was that?" I looked up at him and with horror on my face and a nervous voice I replied, "Sir, I promise you under God that I did not do that on purpose." I told him how I had a "Brain Freeze" and how I did my best to remember the tune to get them out but it was to no avail. I then told him that I decided that I just wouldn't play but I remembered his last words of, "COOPER, "I DON'T CARE WHAT YOU PLAY; YOU JUST GET THEM IN THERE AND GET THEM OUT, THAT'S AN ORDER!"

I then tried to assure him again that I did not do it on purpose and please forgive me.

Chaplain Smith paused for a moment and then said, "Yes, I did give you an order and you followed my orders." He bowed his head and turned and walked away.

My Company Commander and First Sergeant came over and I thought, OH NO!

The Company Commander had a blank look on his face, but at the same time it looked as if he was trying to keep from laughing. The First Sergeant was also trying to hold back laughter.

The First Sergeant spoke up and said, "Cooper, when you played as the Bride and Groom came walking down the aisle, we thought that you had great potential of a music career. But after you played what you did as they left we have a word for you: - "STICK TO YOUR DAY JOB"

And with that, they turned and left.

I felt so bad but there wasn't anything I could do. I turned the organ off, locked up the chapel and left.

Never again was I asked to play at a wedding or anything for that matter. Looking back at that day, what a great - funny memory it has become. I always wondered, what did the Bride and Groom say about that tune and do they look back on that day with disappointment or do they look back with laughter remembering that the Un-Learned, Un-Rehearsed, Very Nervous, Newly Military Wedding Organist, - Chaplain Assistant, played: AULD LANG SYNE!

Auld Lang Syne
(English Translation)

Should *old* acquaintance be forgot,
and never brought to mind ?
Should *old* acquaintance be forgot,
and *old* lang syne ?

CHORUS:
For auld lang syne, my *dear*,
for auld lang syne,
we'll take a cup of kindness yet,
for auld lang syne.

JOKES

IF THERE IS A NEED, THERE IS A WAY

The regular organist for the church retired. A new lady who was going to play in the morning service with hopes of getting the job arrived early to talk to the pastor. The pastor, unable to talk to her because of having to deal with an emergency told the new lady to just do her best and go along with what was happening in the service. After several songs the pastor got up and informed the congregation that the roof needed repairing, there was some plumbing issues that had to be fixed and explained that he needed ten people to stand and give $50 each so that the repairs could get done. He looked over at the new organist and nodded for her to play. She played, The Star Spangled Banner! She got the job!

YOU THINK YOU'RE THE HEAD OF THE HOUSE

You know that the groom at a wedding is going to be a "hen-pecked" husband when the preacher says, "And do you take this women to be your lawfully wedded wife, to love and to hold, for richer - for poorer, through sickness and in health, till death do you part," and the groom looks at his bride and ask, "Do I?"

THE WEDDING

A wide-eyed little girl, attending her first wedding, did not miss a single detail. Afterward she asked her mother: "Did the lady change her mind? She went up the aisle with one man and came back with a different one!"

FINE TUNING

Did you hear about the two radio antennas that got married? The wedding was terrible, but the reception was excellent!

ANNIVERSARY FLOWERS

It was our second anniversary and my husband sent me flowers at the office. He told the florist to write "Happy Anniversary, Year Number 2" on the card. I was thrilled with the flowers, but not so pleased about the card. It read, "Happy Anniversary. You're Number 2."

CLARIFY THAT PLEASE

A local church built a new sanctuary. They moved their very fine old pipe organ from the old sanctuary to the new sanctuary. It was an intricate task that was completed successfully. The local news heralded, "St. Paul Completes Organ Transplant."

HE'S LEARNING FAST!

A young couple came into the church office to fill out a pre-marriage questionnaire form. The young man, who had never talked to a pastor before, was quite nervous and the pastor tried to put him at ease. When they came to the question, 'Are you entering this marriage of your own free will,' there was a long pause. Finally, the girl looked over at the apprehensive young man and said, "Put down yes."

GOOD QUESTION

Attending a wedding for the first time, a little girl whispered to her mother, "Why is the bride dressed in white?" The mother replied, "Because white is the color of happiness, and today is the happiest day of her life." The little girl thought about this for a moment then asked, "So why is the groom wearing black?"

WHO REALLY RUNS THINGS

The man who brags "I run things in my home," usually refers to the lawn mower, the washing machine, the vacuum cleaner, the baby carriage, and errands.

CLEANING UP

One day my housework-challenged husband decided to wash his sweatshirt. Seconds after he stepped into the laundry room, he shouted to me, "What setting do I use on the washing machine?" "It depends," I replied. "What does it say on your shirt" He yelled back, "Atlanta Falcons!"

THINGS DO CHANGE

After church one Sunday two little boys were standing in the church lobby. While they were talking a pretty girl came out of the sanctuary and walked by them.
One of the boys told his friend, "When I quit hating girls, she is going to be the first one that I'm going to quit hating!"

LOOK OUT!

A preacher went to the nursing home to visit for a while. As he went in the front door a little old lady stood there and greeted him by saying, "You look like my 7th husband." The preacher replied, "My word, how many times have you been married?" The lady replied, "SIX!"

CLOSING

Say what? IRS is at the front door, why?
They heard that I got a dollar for being a humorist and comedian so now that puts me in the category of being a professional and now they want to tax me!

Quick, stall them while I go out the back door!

Why?

"I'M GOING TO GO GIVE THIS DOLLAR BACK!"

JOKES

A MODEL

Someone gave me what I thought was a complement; they called me a model comedian. I went home and looked up the word model. The definition of a model is: A replica of the real thing.

CASH EXTRACTION

A boy had swallowed a coin and it got stuck in his throat. His mother ran out in the street yelling for help. A man passing by took the boy by his shoulders and hit him with a few strong strokes on the back, until he coughed the coin out. "I don't know how to thank you, doctor," his mother said. "I'm not a doctor," the man replied. "I'm from the IRS."

INDEX

Gerald L. Cooper, P.O. Box 552, Villa Rica, Ga. 30180 – Author

Contact by Email: circuitridercomedian@gmail.com

Please visit Website at: circuitridercomedian.com

Reid, David. *Leading to the Bedroom, The Christians Couple's Path to Greater Sexual Intimacy and Freedom*, published by InnerMan Resources, 2010, www.InnerMan Resources.com